Korean
한국어 초급부터 중급까지
Language
From the beginning
To the intermediate level

이기선(Kisun Lee)

Korean Language
From the beginning To the intermediate level
한국어 초급부터 중급까지

초판 1쇄 인쇄 2024년 4월 15일
초판 1쇄 발행 2024년 4월 30일

지은이 이기선
펴낸이 서덕일
펴낸곳 도서출판 문예림

출판등록 1962년 7월 12일 (제1962-1호)
주소 경기도 파주시 회동길 366 3층 (10881)
전화 (02) 499-1281~2 **팩스** (02) 499-1283
전자우편 info@moonyelim.com
홈페이지 www.moonyelim.com

ISBN 978-89-7482-937-7 (13710)
값 20,000원

english version

Korean
한국어 초급부터 중급까지
Language

이기선(Kisun Lee)

From the beginning
To the intermediate level

moonyelim

Preface 서문

Preface

North Korea, built under the communist ideology and armed thoroughly with the support of China and the former Soviet Union, unexpectedly invaded the Free Republic of Korea at 04:00 on June 25, 1950. Fortunately, however, thanks to the support of the U.S.-centered UN forces, the Republic of Korea was not conquered by the North Korean military and the Korean War, lasted 3 years, stopped by a cease-fire at 22:00 on July 17, 1953.

I was born the year after the armistice was signed, so I am a person of the generation who has witnessed, heard, and experienced firsthand in Korea the process of changing from the world's poorest country due to the devastation of war to one of the world's top 10 economic powers.

If it had not been for the soldiers from the free countries, led by the United States, who had fought against North Korean and Chinese forces by giving their precious lives in the perilous period just before becoming a communist country, or if my parents had died in the war, or if my parents were residents of North Korea who couldn't escape to South Korea, it would have been impossible to live in today's rich and powerful Korea while enjoying the freedom of life and economic comfort, additionally feeling proud of the country that is getting richer and stronger day by day.

Moreover, recently, many news related to large-scale defense exports are being reported every day as our defense weapons have been recognized for their performance as well as the world's best cost-effectiveness and production capacity across all fields of land, sea and air. As a writer of this book who experienced in charge of ship weapon systems during the design process for the construction of the Korean Navy's new destroyer(KDX Project), and experienced in service as a military attache at the Korean Embassy in Germany for the procurement of foreign weapons from the developed countries in Europe during the active duty days, whenever I hear good news like this, my heart trembles with joy, and cannot help thinking that I am really grateful and happy every day.

In recent years, many young Koreans, including BTS, have shown off their talent to the fullest and are being loved so much by people around the world. At the same time, various aspects of Korean culture and traditions(K-Pop, K-Culture, K-Drama, K-Movie, K-Food, K-Fashion, K-Beauty, K-Weapon, TAEKWONDO, KIMCHI, etc.) that are based on the cultural phenomenon, called Hallyu(Korean Wave), are gaining popularity beyond the boundaries of region, ideology and religion. In June of Yr. 2022, 18-year-old Yunchan Lim became the youngest winner in the 60-year history of the Van Cliburn International Piano Competition held in the United States. He was praised as a genius pianist that there could be only one person per century and greatly showed off the excellence of Koreans. Theses phenomena naturally amplifies the interest in Korea and the desire to learn Korean.

A language is an intangible outcome of a nation or a country for thousands of years of life style, mind-set, natural environment, family relations, religion, social structure, relationship with surrounding forces, history of state formation, ongoing changes in society, technological developments etc. Therefore, the letter or character which consists of alphabets and is a vessel of language, not only quickly spreads all tangible and intangible products to human societies but also conveys them to the future generations. In addition, the letters are really important means for understanding the rise and fall of a country or nation in the past and predicting the future. Therefore, learning and understanding another language is the surest and fastest way to know the people and country using that language.

Preface

It is no exaggeration to say that one of the main causes of the current development of the whole society, including technology, culture, etc. and the growth of national economy in Korea is the Korean alphabet consisted of 10 vowels and 14 consonants. Since Korean alphabet is simpler than any other in the world, it is possible to read Korean letters with almost accurate pronunciation just by studying it for a day or two. In addition, Hangeul-alphabet is the simplest and most flexible of all the alphabets in which the phonemic alphabet consisting of the smallest phonetic unit is used. One more additional advantage that there are only 24 alphabets in Hangeul, otherwise such as English and Japanese, one alphabet is written in two ways, as capital letter and small letter of English and Katakana and Hiragana of Japanese, so the total number of alphabets is 52 in English and 92 in Japanese. Therefore, all sounds that can be heard by the human ear can be written in the most similar and convenient way by using Hangeul-alphabets moreover it can be used more conveniently than any other alphabet for the digitalized communication of information that is the heart of modern technology due to the minimized number of alphabets.

This study book explains the characteristics and structure of Korean in English as much detail as possible using the standardized grammar system. In addition, the sentences that frequently appear in everyday life are used for example sentences, and the supplementary explanations are provided as necessary to facilitate understanding of the usage of colloquial style that is difficult for foreigners to understand. Therefore, English-speaking people who are learning Korean for the first time can systematically study the Korean language ranging from basic to intermediate levels by themselves.

January 2024(Yr. of Dragon), written by the author.

Preface 서문

공산주의 이념으로 건립된 북한은 중국과 옛 소련의 지원을 받아 철저히 무장하여 1950년 6월 25일 04시에 자유 대한민국을 기습적으로 남침하였다. 그러나 다행스럽게도 미군을 중심으로 하는 UN군의 지원 덕분에 대한민국은 북한군에 정복되지 않았고, 3년간 지속된 한국전쟁은 1953년 7월 17일 22시에 휴전으로 멈추었다.

필자는 휴전협정이 맺어진 그다음 해에 태어났으므로 전쟁의 황폐화로 인한 지구상 최하위 빈곤 국가에서부터 지금은 세계 10대 경제 대국에 포함되는 국가로 변화해 가는 과정을 직접 보고 듣고 경험하면서 살아온 세대의 한 사람이다.

만약에, 미국을 주축으로 하는 자유 국가들의 군인들이 공산화 직전의 아슬아슬했던 시기에 귀중한 생명을 바쳐가면서 북한군과 중공군을 상대로 싸워주지 않았더라면, 또는 필자의 부모가 전쟁 통에 사망했더라면, 아니면 나의 부모가 남한으로 탈출하지 못한 북한의 주민이었다면, 지금의 부강한 대한민국에서 삶의 자유와 경제적인 여유를 누리면서, 여기에 덤으로 나날이 부강해지는 조국에 대한 자부심까지 느끼면서 사는 것은 불가능했을 것이다.

더구나, 최근에는 육해공 전 분야에 걸쳐서 우리의 방산 무기가 성능뿐만 아니라 세계 최고의 가성비와 생산능력을 인정받아 대형 방산 수출과 관련된 많은 뉴스가 연일 전해지고 있다. 현역시절, 한국해군의 신형구축함 건조(KDX 사업)를 위한 설계과정에서 함정무기체계 관련 주무담당자로서, 그리고 주독일 한국대사관에서 무관으로 근무하면서 유럽 선진국으로부터 외국산 무기 조달 업무를 경험했던 필자로서, 이런 희소식을 접할 때마다 가슴이 떨려오는 희열과 함께 하루하루가 정말 고맙고 행복하다는 생각을 금할 수 없다.

최근 들어서 방탄소년단(BTS)을 비롯한 수많은 대한민국의 젊은이들이 그들의 실력을 마음껏 과시하여 세계인들로부터 열화와 같은 사랑을 받고 있다. 이와 함께 다방면에 걸친 대한민국의 문화와 전통이 한류(Hallyu: Korean Wave)라는 문화적 현상을 기반으로 하여 K-Pop, K-Culture, K-Drama, K-Movie, K-Food, K-Fashion, K-Beauty, K-Weapon, TAEKWONDO, KIMCHI 등의 이름으로 지역, 이념, 종교의 벽을 넘어서 대단한 인기를 끌고 있다. 2022년 6월에는 18세 임윤찬 군이 미국에서 열린 반 클라이번 국제 피아노 콩쿠르에서 60년 역사상 최연소우승을 차지하였다. 윤찬 군은 한 세기에 한 명 정도 나올 수 있다는 천재 피아니스트로 칭송을 받으면서

Preface

한국인의 우수성을 크게 과시하였다. 이러한 현상들은 자연스럽게 한국에 관한 관심과 더불어 한국어를 배우고자 하는 열망을 증폭시킨다.

언어는 하나의 민족 또는 국가에서 수 천 년에 걸친 생활과 사고방식, 자연환경, 가족관계, 종교, 사회구조, 주변 세력과의 관계, 국가가 형성된 역사, 진행 중인 사회의 변화, 기술 발전 등, 모든 것들이 융화되어 나타나는 무형의 결과물이다. 따라서 알파벳으로 형성되고, 언어를 담는 그릇인 글자는 모든 유무형의 산물을 인류사회에 신속하게 파급할 뿐만 아니라 후세에 전하는 기능을 갖기 때문에 글자는 한 국가나 민족이 겪었던 과거의 흥망성쇠를 이해할 수 있으며, 미래까지도 예측할 수 있는 정말 중요한 수단이다. 그러므로 다른 언어를 배워서 이해한다는 것은 그 언어를 사용하는 민족과 국가를 가장 확실하고 빠르게 알 수 있는 길이다.

현재의 대한민국에서 나타나는 기술, 문화 등을 포함하는 사회 전반의 발전과 성장하는 국가 경제의 주요 원인 중 하나가 바로 10개의 모음과 14개의 자음으로 구성된 한글자모라고 해도 과언이 아니다. 한글자모는 세계의 어느 문자보다 단순하므로 하루 이틀만 공부해도 거의 정확한 발음으로 한글을 읽을 수 있다. 또한, 한글은 음성학적 최소단위의 음소문자가 사용되는 모든 문자 중에서도 가장 단순하고 유연하다. 한글의 추가적인 장점은 영어의 대문자와 소문자, 일본어의 카타까나와 히라가나처럼 하나의 문자를 두 가지로 사용하기 때문에 전체적인 문자의 숫자는 영어 52개, 일본어 92개가 되지만, 한글자모는 24개뿐이라는 것이다. 그러므로 한글자모는 인간의 귀로 들을 수 있는 모든 소리를 가장 편리하고 유사하게 글자로 표기할 수 있을 뿐만 아니라, 24개뿐이라는 최소화된 자모의 숫자로 인해 현대 기술의 핵심이라고 할 수 있는 디지털체계의 정보소통에도 어느 문자보다 편리하게 사용될 수 있다.

본 학습서는 한국어의 특성과 구조에 관해 정형화된 문법체계를 이용하여 가능한 상세하게 영어로 설명하였다. 또한, 예문은 일상생활에 자주 등장하는 문장을 사용하였으며, 외국인들에게 어렵게 느껴지는 구어체 활용에 대해서도 이해가 쉽게 필요에 따라 보충설명 하였다. 따라서 한국어를 처음 배우는 영어권 출신자들이 기초부터 중급 수준에 이르는 내용을 혼자서도 체계적으로 공부할 수 있다.

2024년(갑진년) 1월, 저자 씀

History and characteristics of Hangeul-alphabet
한글자모의 역사와 특성

History and Characteristics of Hangeul-alphabet

The Korean language is called as Hangugeo(한국어) and the letters of Korean language are called as Hangeul(한글). The alphabet of Hangeul was created in year 1443(26th years of Sejong) by King Sejong the Great as the 4th King of the Choson Dynasty. And in September 1446, Hangeul, based on a new alphabetic system, was promulgated as the official national script through the book titled "Hunminjeongeum(The Korean script)".

Before the creation of Hangeul-alphabet, not only all the national records but also the personal correspondences were written in Chinese characters which are called as Hanja of word-alphabet. At that time, the children of the upper-class family spent all their youth studying Chinese characters and literature from an early age because the people could not become intellectuals or government officials without knowing the Chinese characters and literature. Therefore, it was nearly impossible for the children of the lower class family to acquire knowledge through the academic study.

A character of Hanja is an alphabet that has its own meaning as a self-reliable word. The number of Chinese characters was recently announced at 53,000, so more than 30,000 can be estimated for that time. Considering that this number of alphabets is beyond human ability to be well aware of, so we can guess how difficult it is to learn Chinese letters and literature.

History and characteristics of Hangeul-alphabet
한글자모의 역사와 특성

King Sejong the Great created the 28-alphabets personally by demonstrating his genius, based on the spirit of loving the people to eliminate the difficulties of the common people suffering from the effects of illiteracy because they could not learn Hanja. This new alphabetic system is not only the most original and scientific in the history of alphabets of the world, but it presents also the subtlety about the formation of the universe. It is also the only alphabet with a record of all the steps of creation from the beginning with nothing missing. The most scientific alphabet means that all sounds from all natures, including human-being can be recorded more similar than any other alphabets on the world due to the unique flexibility of pronunciation. However, Japanese, which is in the same Chinese character region but uses the syllabic character that is lacking in flexibility for pronunciation as its alphabet, must use Chinese characters together because of its many homonyms, but Korean language mostly can be perfectly understood with just pure Hangeul due to its unrivaled flexibility of pronunciation.

The consonants have the root in the structures of the lips, teeth, tongue, and throat that are related with human voice, and the vowels are made up of a combination of three elements of universe which are heaven, earth and human-being in between. Four of the first 28 alphabets ceased to exist, so 24 alphabets(14 consonants and 10 vowels) are currently used as the basic alphabets in Hangeul.

History and Characteristics of Hangeul-alphabet

한국의 언어를 한국어라 하고 한국어에 사용되는 문자를 한글이라고 한다. 한글에 사용되는 자모는 1443년(세종 26년), 조선왕조의 제3대 임금 세종대왕에 의해 창제되었다. 그리고 1446년 9월 새로운 자모체계의 한글을 훈민정음이라는 제목의 책을 통하여 국가의 공식적인 문자로 반포하였다.

한글 문자가 반포되기 이전에는 국가의 모든 기록물뿐만 아니라 개인 서신까지도 중국의 문자인 한자가 사용되었다. 당시에는 한자를 모르면 지식인이나 정부의 관리가 될 수 없었기 때문에 양반계급의 자제는 어릴 때부터 한자와 한문을 배우느라 젊은 시간을 전부 허비하는 형국이었다. 따라서 하층계급의 자제들에게 삶에 유용한 지식을 쌓기 위한 체계적인 학문의 공부는 엄두조차 내기 어려웠다.

한자의 한 글자는 하나의 알파벳이면서 동시에 고유의 의미를 갖는 독립된 단어다. 최근 중국 한자의 숫자가 53,000여 개로 발표된 것으로 보아, 당시에도 최소 30,000개는 넘었을 것으로 추측할 수 있다. 이 알파벳의 숫자가 인간의 능력으로서는 모두 숙지할 수 없는 양이라는 것을 고려하면 한자와 한문 공부의 고초가 얼마나 컸을지 짐작할 수 있다.

세종대왕은 한자를 배우지 못해 문맹의 폐해에 시달리는 다수의 평민이 겪는 어려움을 없애기 위해 애민정신을 바탕으로 한 천재성을 발휘하여 28자의 자모를 몸소 창제하였다. 이 새로운 자모체계는 세계 알파벳 역사상 가장 독창적이고 과학적일 뿐만 아니라 우주의 형성에 대한 미묘함도 보여 준다. 또한, 자모를 창안해가는 단계가 시작부터 고스란히 기록되어 있는 유일한 알파벳이다. 가장 과학적인 자모라는 의미는 인간을 포함한 모든 피조물의 소리와 형태를 어느 문자보다 더 유사하게 기록할 수 있다는 발음의 독보적인 유연성을 뜻한다. 그러나 같은 한자권이지만 유연성이 부족한 음절문자를 알파벳으로 사용하는 일본어는 많은 동음이의어 때문에 한자를 함께 사용하여야 하지만, 한국어는 탁월한 발음의 유연성 덕분에 순수한 한글만으로도 대부분 완벽하게 이해할 수 있다.

자음은 인간의 발성과 관계되는 입술, 치아, 혀, 목구멍의 구조로부터 만들어졌고, 모음은 하늘과 땅, 그 사이에 있는 인간이라는 3개 요소를 조합하여 만들어졌다. 최초의 28개 자모 중 4개는 소멸하고 현재 24개의 자모(자음 14개, 모음 10개)가 한글의 기본 자모로 사용되고 있다.

목차

Contents

SECTION

01 한글 자모와 발음

Hangeul-alphabet and Pronunciation

1. Basic Hangeul-alphabets

Consonant [Reading]		Vowel [Reading]	
ㄱ	[giyeok]	ㅏ	[a]
ㄴ	[nieun]	ㅑ	[ya]
ㄷ	[digeut]	ㅓ	[eo]
ㄹ	[rieul]	ㅕ	[yeo]
ㅁ	[mieum]	ㅗ	[o]
ㅂ	[bieup]	ㅛ	[yo]
ㅅ	[siot]	ㅜ	[u]
ㅇ	[ieung]	ㅠ	[yu]
ㅈ	[jieut]	ㅡ	[eu]
ㅊ	[chieut]	ㅣ	[i]
ㅋ	[kieuk]		
ㅌ	[tieut]		
ㅍ	[pieup]		
ㅎ	[hieut]		

alphabet
알파벳[alpabet]
자모[jamo]

pronunciation
발음[bareum]

consonant
자음[jaeum]

vowel
모음[moeum]

reading
읽기[ilkki]

letter/character
문자[munjja]
글자[geuljja]

Note 1

The 14 consonants are divided according to the position in the mouth where the sound is generated.

(1) Molar sound(아음[aeum]): ㄱ, ㅋ

(2) Lingual sound(설음[seoreum]): ㄴ, ㄷ, ㅌ, ㄹ

(3) Labial sound(순음[suneum]): ㅁ, ㅂ, ㅍ

(4) Dental sound(치음[chieum]): ㅅ, ㅈ, ㅊ

(5) Guttural sound(후음[hueum]): ㅇ, ㅎ

Note 2

The vowels are divided based on the attribute.

(1) Positive: ㅏ, ㅑ, ㅗ, ㅛ

(2) Negative: ㅓ, ㅕ, ㅜ, ㅠ, ㅡ

(3) Neutral: ㅣ

Note 3

One letter of Hangeul which is one syllable(음절[eumjeol]) is made up in two ways.

(1) Initial sound(초성[choseong]: 자음) + Final sound(종성[jongseong]: 모음)

(2) Initial sound(초성: 자음) + Medial sound(중성[jungseong]: 모음) + Final sound(종성: 자음)

※ 자음 of the initial sound is called as the initial consonant.

※ 자음 of the final sound is called as the final consonant(받침자음[batchimjaeum]).

※ When a syllable has "ㅇ" as an initial consonant, the part("ㅇ" + 모음) is called as a medial vowel(중간모음[jungganmoeum]).

2. Combination of 모음 and 자음 for basic syllables(음절)

	ㅏ	ㅑ	ㅓ	ㅕ	ㅗ	ㅛ	ㅜ	ㅠ	ㅡ	ㅣ
ㄱ	가 [GA]	갸 [GYA]	거 [GEO]	겨 [GYEO]	고 [GO]	교 [GYO]	구 [GU]	규 [GYU]	그 [GEU]	기 [GI]
ㄴ	나 [NA]	냐 [NYA]	너 [NEO]	녀 [NYEO]	노 [NO]	뇨 [NYO]	누 [NU]	뉴 [NYU]	느 [NEU]	니 [NI]
ㄷ	다 [DA]	댜 [DYA]	더 [DEO]	뎌 [DYEO]	도 [DO]	됴 [DYO]	두 [DU]	듀 [DYU]	드 [DEU]	디 [DI]
ㄹ	라 [RA]	랴 [RYA]	러 [REO]	려 [RYEO]	로 [RO]	료 [RYO]	루 [RU]	류 [RYU]	르 [REU]	리 [RI]
ㅁ	마 [MA]	먀 [MYA]	머 [MEO]	며 [MYEO]	모 [MO]	묘 [MYO]	무 [MU]	뮤 [MYU]	므 [MEU]	미 [MI]
ㅂ	바 [BA]	뱌 [BYA]	버 [BEO]	벼 [BYEO]	보 [BO]	뵤 [BYO]	부 [BU]	뷰 [BYU]	브 [BEU]	비 [BI]
ㅅ	사 [SA]	샤 [SYA]	서 [SEO]	셔 [SYEO]	소 [SO]	쇼 [SYO]	수 [SU]	슈 [SYU]	스 [SEU]	시 [SI]
ㅇ	아 [A]	야 [YA]	어 [EO]	여 [YEO]	오 [O]	요 [YO]	우 [U]	유 [YU]	으 [EU]	이 [I]
ㅈ	자 [JA]	쟈 [JYA]	저 [JEO]	져 [JYEO]	조 [JO]	죠 [JYO]	주 [JU]	쥬 [JYU]	즈 [JEU]	지 [JI]
ㅊ	차 [CHA]	챠 [CHYA]	처 [CHEO]	쳐 [SHYEO]	초 [CHO]	쵸 [CHYO]	추 [CHU]	츄 [CHYU]	츠 [CHEU]	치 [CHI]
ㅋ	카 [KA]	캬 [KYA]	커 [KEO]	켜 [KYEO]	코 [KO]	쿄 [KYO]	쿠 [KU]	큐 [KYU]	크 [KEU]	키 [KI]
ㅌ	타 [TA]	탸 [TYA]	터 [TEO]	텨 [TYEO]	토 [TO]	툐 [TYO]	투 [TU]	튜 [TYU]	트 [TEU]	티 [TI]
ㅍ	파 [PA]	퍄 [PYA]	퍼 [PEO]	펴 [PYEO]	포 [PO]	표 [PYO]	푸 [PU]	퓨 [PYU]	프 [PEU]	피 [PI]
ㅎ	하 [HA]	햐 [HYA]	허 [HEO]	혀 [HYEO]	호 [HO]	효 [HYO]	후 [HU]	휴 [HYU]	흐 [HEU]	히 [HI]

3. Pronunciation of alphabet

1 Vowel(모음)

구분
classification

단모음
The shape of the lips or the tongue does not change while pronouncing.

구분[gubun]*	모음	발음	example (예[ye]) of words	
Single Vowel 단모음 [danmoeum]	ㅏ	a	아버지 [abeoji]	father
	ㅑ	ya	야구 [yagu]	baseball
	ㅓ	eo	어머니 [eomeoni]	mother
	ㅕ	yeo	여행 [yeohaeng]	travel, trip
	ㅗ	o	오리 [ori]	duck
	ㅛ	yo	요리 [yori]	dish, food, cooking
	ㅜ	u	우산 [usan]	umbrella
	ㅠ	yu	유치원 [yuchiwon]	kindergarten
	ㅡ	eu	으깨다 [eukkaeda]	crush
	ㅣ	i	이발소 [ibalsso]	barbershop
	ㅐ(ㅏ+ㅣ)	ae	애국가 [aegukkka]	national anthem

구분[gubun]*	모음	발음	example (예[ye]) of words	
	ㅔ(ㅓ+ㅣ)	e	에너지 [eneoji]	energy
	ㅚ(ㅗ+ㅣ)	oe	외국 [oeguk]	foreign country
	ㅟ(ㅜ+ㅣ)	wi	위험 [wiheom]	danger
Double Vowel 이중모음 [ijungmoeum]	ㅒ(ㅑ+ㅣ)	yae	얘기 [yaegi] * Abbreviated word of "이야기"	story, talk
	ㅖ(ㅕ+ㅣ)	ye	예절 [yejeol]	etiquette
	ㅢ*(ㅡ+ㅣ)	eui, i	의사 [euisa]	doctor
			희망 [himang]	hope
			무늬 [muni]	pattern, figure
	ㅘ(ㅗ+ㅏ)	wa	과일 [gwail]	fruit
	ㅙ(ㅗ+ㅐ)	wae	괭이 [gwaengi]	hoe
	ㅝ(ㅜ+ㅓ)	wo	원숭이 [wonsungi]	monkey
	ㅞ(ㅜ+ㅔ)	we	궤도 [gwedo]	rail

이중모음
The shape of the lips or the tongue changes while pronouncing.

ㅢ
"ㅢ" is pronounced by [i] of single vowel when the initial consonant is not "ㅇ".

2 Consonant(자음)

구분	자음	발음	예	
Single Consonant 단자음 [danjaeum]	ㄱ	g, k	국[guk]	soup, broth
	ㄴ	n	나비[nabi]	butterfly
	ㄷ	d, t	돼지 [dwaeji]	pig
			곧[got]	soon
	ㄹ	r, l	라디오 [radio]	radio
			골짜기 [goljjagi]	valley
	ㅁ	m	말 [mal]	horse, language, speech
	ㅂ	b, p	밥 [bap]	boiled rice, meal, food
	ㅅ	s, t	사랑 [sarang]	love
			붓[but]	writing brush
	ㅇ	-, ng	아이[ai]	child
			양말 [yangmal]	socks
	ㅈ	j, t	자전거 [jajeongeo]	bicycle
			잦다 [jatdda]	frequent
	ㅊ	ch, t	창문 [changmun]	window
			숯[sut]	charcoal
	ㅋ	k	콩나물 [kongnamul]	bean sprouts
	ㅌ	t	태양 [taeyang]	sun
	ㅍ	p	팔다 [palda]	sell
	ㅎ	h	화장실 [hwajangsil]	rest-room, W.C.

구분	자음	발음	예	
Twin Consonant 쌍자음 [ssangjaeum]	ㄲ	kk	꽃 [kkot]	flower
	ㄸ	dd	땀 [ddam]	sweat
	ㅃ	bb	아빠 [abba]	daddy
			오빠 [obba]	elder brother of girl
	ㅆ	ss	싸움 [ssaum]	quarrel, scuffle, fight
	ㅉ	jj	짜다 [jjada]	salty, weave, squeeze
Final Double Consonant 겹받침 [gyeopbatchim]	ㄳ	k	넋 [neok]	soul
	ㄵ	n	앉다 [andda]	sit down
	ㄶ	n	많다 [manta]	many, much
	ㄺ	k*	닭 [dak]	chicken
	ㄻ	m*	굶다 [gumdda]	skip a meal, starve
	ㄼ	p*	밟다 [bapdda]	step on
		l	넓다 [neoldda]	wide, broad, spacious
	ㄽ	l	외곬 [oegol]	one-track mind
	ㄾ	l	핥다 [haldda]	lick
	ㄿ	p*	읊다 [eupdda]	read, recite
	ㅀ	l	싫다 [silta]	dislike, be disagreeable
	ㅄ	p	값 [gap]	price

* Pronounced by the latter consonant of 겹받침.

- Reading of twin consonant

  - ㄲ: 쌍기역[ssanggiyeok]
  - ㄸ: 쌍디귿[ssangdigeut]
  - ㅃ: 쌍비읍[ssangbieup]
  - ㅆ: 쌍시옷[ssangsiot]
  - ㅉ: 쌍지읒[ssangjieut]

- In Hangeul-alphabet, all vowels are voiced sounds made by the vibration of vocal cords. Four of the consonants(ㄴ, ㅁ, ㄹ, ㅇ) are voiced consonants, and the remaining ten are voiceless consonants that do not cause the vocal cords to vibrate.

  - voiced sound: 유성음[yuseongeum]
  - voiced consonant: 유성자음[yuseongjaeum]
  - voiceless sound: 무성음[museongeum]
  - voiceless consonant: 무성자음[museongjaeum]

- 자음 is divided into three groups except for nasal consonants(ㄴ, ㅁ, ㅇ), a voiceless frictional consonant(ㅎ) and a flowing consonant(ㄹ).

  - Plain sound(평음[pyeongeum]): ㄱ, ㄷ, ㅂ, ㅅ, ㅈ
  - Strong(Fortis) sound(경음[gyeongeum]): ㄲ, ㄸ, ㅃ, ㅆ, ㅉ
  - Aspirate sound(격음[gyeogeum]): ㅋ, ㅌ, ㅍ, ㅊ

- Usage of consonant

  - 겹받침 can not be used as an initial consonant.
  - All of 자음 except "ㄸ", "ㅃ" and "ㅉ" are used as 받침자음.
  - The pronunciation of 받침자음 is one of "ㄱ[k]", "ㄴ[n]", "ㄷ[t]", "ㄹ[l]", "ㅁ[m]", "ㅂ[p]" and "ㅇ[ng]".

Gramatical terms

- 자모[jamo]: Korean alphabet
- 받침자음[batchimjaeum]: final consonant
- 겹받침[gyeopbatchim]: final double consonant
- 음절[eumjeol]: syllable
- 중간모음[jungganmoeum]: medial vowel
- 문장[munjang]: sentence
- 단어[daneo], 낱말[nanmal]: word
- 한국어[hanggugeo], 한국말[hanggungmal]: Korean language
- 영어[yeongeo]: English
- 준말[junmal]: abbreviated word
- 본딧말[bondinmal]: original word

3 Sequence of strokes of each 자모

1 모음

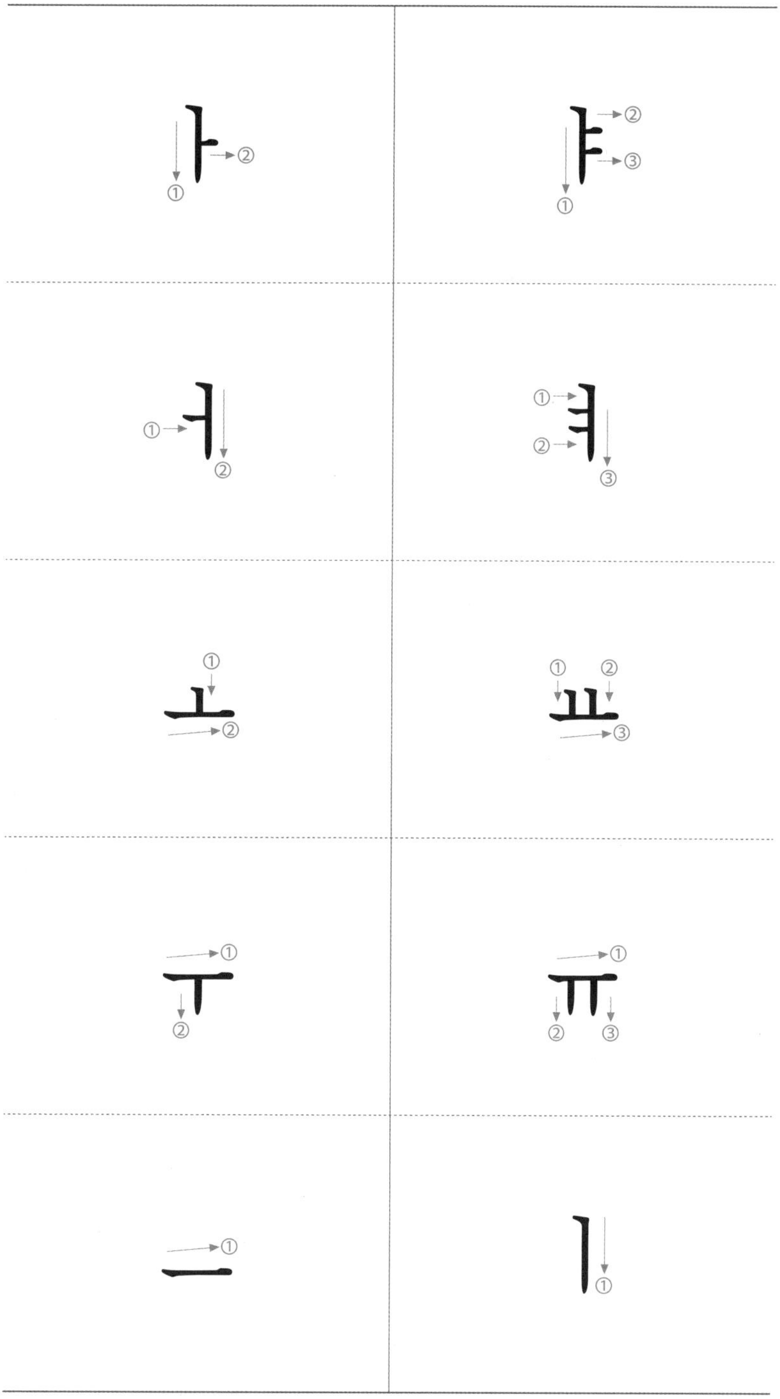

2 자음

ㄱ	ㄴ
ㄷ	ㄹ
ㅁ	ㅂ
ㅅ	ㅇ
ㅈ	ㅊ
ㅋ	ㅌ
ㅍ	ㅎ

4 Sequence of 자모 of a letter

Examples: "타", "옴", "값" and "뚫"

타	ㅌ	타		
옴	ㅇ	오	옴	
값	ㄱ	가	갑	값
뚫	ㄸ	뚜	뚤	뚫

SECTION

02 단어 읽기 규칙

Rules for Reading Words

In order to read Korean sentences exactly,
it is necessary to know first the rules of pronunciation of words.

1. Liaison of 받침자음 to "ㅇ": 연음법칙[yeoneumbeopchik]

example
예[ye]

meaning
뜻[ddeut], 의미[euimi]

When preceding 음절 with 받침자음 is followed by 음절 with 중간모음, the pronunciation of 받침자음 becomes the initial sound of the following 음절.

예	발음	뜻[ddeut]
언어	[eoneo: 어너]	language
음악	[eumak: 으막]	music
한국어	[hanggugeo: 항구거]	Korean language
부엌에	[bueoke: 부어케]	in kitchen
문어	[muneo: 무너]	octopus

2. Neutralization of pronunciation: 중화법칙[junghwabeopchik]

받침자음 according to the phonetic attribute is pronounced one of "ㅋ[k]", "ㅌ[t]" and "ㅍ[p]" which are sounds of glottal stop as follows.

ㄱ, ㅋ, ㄲ	→	ㅋ[k]
먹다	[meokdda: 먹따]	eat
부엌	[bueok: 부억]	kitchen
밖	[bak: 박]	outside

ㄷ, ㅅ, ㅆ, ㅈ, ㅊ, ㅌ, ㅎ		→ ㅌ[t]
듣다	[deutdda: 듣따]	hear
맛	[mat: 맡]	taste
갔다	[gatdda: 같따]	went
젖다	[jeotdda: 젇따]	wet
꽃	[kkot: 꼳]	flower
솥	[sot: 솥]	kettle
히읗	[hieut: 히읕]	ㅎ

ㅂ, ㅍ		→ ㅍ[p]
밥	[bap: 밮]	boiled rice
숲	[sup: 숲]	forest

3. Nasalization: 비음화[bieumhwa]

1 비음화 of 받침자음

Due to the phonetic matching of 자음, when the initial consonant of the following 음절 is the nasal consonant(ㄴ, ㅁ, ㅇ), 받침자음 of the preceding 음절 is also pronounced nasally.

ㄱ, ㅋ		→ ㅇ
한국말	[hanggungmal: 한궁말]	Korean language
부엌문	[bueongmun: 부엉문]	door of kitchen
막내	[mangnae: 망내]	the youngest child

ㄷ, ㅌ		→ ㄴ
믿는다	[minneunda: 민는다]	present tense of "믿다 (believe)"
낱말	[nanmal: 난말]	word

ㅂ		→ ㅁ
갑니다.	[gamnida:감니다]	honorific expression of "가다(go)"

ㅅ, ㅈ, ㅊ, ㅆ		→ ㄴ
솟는(←솟다)	[sonneun:손는]	rising(pre-noun)
젖는(←젖다)	[jeonneun:전는]	getting wet(pre-noun)
꽃나무	[kkonnamu:꼰나무]	tree of flower
있는(←있다)	[inneun:인는]	existing(pre-noun)

ㅎ		→ ㄴ
놓는(←놓다)	[nonneun:논는]	putting(pre-noun)

2 비음화 from "ㄹ" to "ㄴ"

When the preceding 음절 has any 받침자음 except for "ㄴ" and "ㄹ", the initial consonant(ㄹ) of the following 음절 is pronounced "ㄴ".

항로	[hangno: 항노]	sailing route, aerial route
독립	[dongnip: 동닙]	independence
심리	[simni: 심니]	psychology
정류장	[jeongnyujang: 정뉴장]	stop for bus or taxi
대학로	[daehangno: 대항노]	way for university
국립묘지	[gungnipmyoji: 궁닙묘지]	national cemetery

4. Change to strong sound: 경음화[gyeongeumhwa]

The initial consonant is pronounced strong(fortis) behind 음절 which has any 받침자음 except for "ㄴ", "ㄹ", "ㅇ" and "ㅎ".

먹다	[meokdda: 먹따]	eat
꽃밭	[kkotbbat: 꼳빧]	flower bed
학생	[hakssaeng: 학쌩]	student
갚다	[gapdda: 갑따]	pay
앉다	[andda: 안따]	sit down
씻다	[ssitdda: 씯따]	wash
젊다	[jeomdda: 점따]	young
검다	[geomdda: 검따]	black
넓고 짧다	[neolkko jjaldda: 널꼬 짤따]	wide and short
학교	[hakkkyo: 학꾜]	school

5. Change to aspirate sound: 격음화[gyeokeumhwa]

When 자음(ㅎ) of preceding or following 음절 is mixed with the plain consonant(ㄱ, ㄷ, ㅂ, ㅈ), theses are pronounced aspirate(ㅋ, ㅌ, ㅍ, ㅊ).

좋다	[jota: 조타]	good
많다	[manta: 만타]	many, much
국화	[gukwa: 구콰]	national flower, chrysanthemum
입학	[ipak: 이팍]	admission to a school
놓다	[nota: 노타]	put down
앉히다	[anchida: 안치다]	seat
맏형	[matyeong: 마텽]	the eldest brother

6. Palatalization: 구개음화[gugaeeumhwa]

음절 of "이" or "히" is pronounced "지" or "치" if the preceding 음절 has 받침자음 of "ㄷ" or "ㅌ".

같이	[gachi: 가치]	together
해돋이	[haedoji: 해도지]	sun rising
굳이	[guji: 구지]	firmly, stubbonly
굳히다	[guchida: 구치다]	harden, coagulate
묻히다	[muchida: 무치다]	be buried
맏이	[maji: 마지]	the first child

7. Omission of "ㅎ": "ㅎ" 생략[hieut saengryak]

The pronunciation of "ㅎ" which is 받침자음 is omitted when the following 음절 has 중간모음.

좋아요.	[joayo: 조아요]	honorific expression of "좋다(good)"
많아요.	[manayo: 마나요]	honorific expression of "많다(many/much)"
좋은	[joeun: 조은]	good(pre-noun)
많은	[maneun: 마는]	many/much(pre-noun)

8. Rule for pronunciation of the initial consonant: 두음법칙[dueumbeopchik]

"ㄴ" and "ㄹ" cannot be used for the initial consonant of the initial syllable of a word, instead "ㅇ" is used.

녀자 → 여자 [yeoja]	woman
년말 → 연말 [yeonmal]	the end of the year
료리 → 요리 [yori]	food, cooking, dish
닉명 → 익명 [ikmyeong]	anonymity, pseudonym
리유 → 이유 [iyu]	reason

- This rule is not applicable to the words of foreign origin except Chinese origin when written by Korean letters.

라면	[ramyeon]	ramyon, instant noodle
라디오	[radio]	radio
라틴	[ratin]	Latin

SECTION

03 일상 관용표현

Daily Idiomatic Expressions

Let's learn daily idiomatic expressions in order to practice reading sentences and to understand some idiomatic expressions in 한국어.

This greeting is used regardless of time and also used when meeting as well as parting.

☐ **안녕!**[annyeong]
Good morning(afternoon/evening)!
Good-bye!

☐ **아저씨, 안녕하세요!**[ajeossi annyeonghaseyo]
Good morning(afternoon/evening), uncle!
How are you, uncle?

☐ **안녕하십니까?**[annyeonghasimnikka]
Good morning(afternoon/evening), sir!
How are you, madam?

☐ **만나서 반갑습니다.**
Nice to meet you, sir!

☐ **할머니, 어떻게 지내세요?**[halmeoni eoddeoke jinaeseyo]
How are you, grandma?

The inflections of word-ending(~요., ~요?, ~요!, ~ㅂ니까?, ~ㅂ니다.) are the honorific expressions. If there is no honorific word-ending, the sentence is a non-honorific expression. (→ Section 8, Note)

☐ **계십니까?**[gyesimnikka]
Anybody home, sir?
Excuse me, sir?

☐ **안녕히 계세요.**[annyeonghi gyeseyo] *Leaving guest to host
Good-bye, Mr. ~.

☐ **안녕히 가세요.**[annyeonghi gaseyo] *Host to leaving guest
Good-bye, Mrs. ~.

☐ **고마워.**[gomawo]
Thank you!

☐ **감사합니다.**[gamsahamnida] / **고맙습니다.**[gomapsseumnida]
Thank you, madam.

☐ **천만에!**[cheonmane]
You are welcome! / Not at all!

☐ **천만에요.**[cheonmaneyo]
Not at all, Mr. ~! / You are welcome, Mrs. ~!

☐ 미안해. [mianhae]
Sorry!

☐ 사장님, 미안합니다./죄송합니다.
[sajangnim, mianhamnida/joisonghamnida]
President, I'm sorry, sir!

☐ 용서해 줘. [yongseohae jwo]
Forgive me!

☐ 용서해 주세요. [yongseohae juseyo]
Forgive me, Miss ~!

☐ 잠깐 기다리세요. [jamkkan gidariseyo]
Wait a moment, auntie!

☐ 잠깐만. [jamkkanman]
Moment please!

☐ 조심하십시오. [josimhasipsiyo]
Be careful, sir!

☐ 조심하세요. [josimhaseyo]
Be careful, mom!

☐ 조심해. [josimhae]
Be careful.

☐ 뭐 해?/하니? [mwo hae/hani] (→ Section 9, Interrogative sentence)
What are you doing?

☐ 아빠, 뭐 하세요? [abba mwo haseyo]
What are you doing, daddy?

☐ 알겠습니까? [algesseumnikka]
Did you understand, madam?

☐ 예, 알겠습니다. [ye algesseumnida]
Yes, sir. I understood.

☐ 아니요, 모르겠습니다. [aniyo moreugesseumnida]
No, sir. I don't understand./I don't know.

□ 알겠어?/알겠니?[algesseo/algenni]
Understood?

□ 모르겠어?/모르겠니?[moreugesseo/moreugenni]
Don't you know?(Don't you understand?)

□ 응[eung], 알겠어.
Yes, understood.

□ 아니, 모르겠어.[ani moreugesseo]
No, I don't know.(I don't understand.)

□ 몰라.[mola]
I don't know.

□ 모르겠습니다.[moreumnida]
I don't know, sir.

□ 싫어.[sireo]
I don't like.

□ 싫어요.[sireoyo]
I don't like, grandma.

□ 자기야, 사랑해![jagiya, saranghae]
Love you, my darling!

□ 사랑해요.[saranghaeyo]
I love you, dear.

□ 사랑합니다.[saranghamnida]
I love you, Miss ~.

□ 신사, 숙녀 여러분, 모두 사랑합니다.
[sinsa sungnyeonyeoreobun modu saranghamnida]
Ladies and gentlemen, I love you all.

□ 나 너 좋아해.[na neo joahae]
I like you.

□ 너 나 좋아해?[neo na joahae]
Do you like me?

☐ 이거 얼마예요?[igeo eolmayeyo]
How much is this, Mr. ~?

☐ 이거 얼마야?/얼마니?[igeo eolmaya/eolmani]
How much is this?

☐ 지금 몇시예요?[jigeum myeotsiyeyo]
What time is it, Mr. ~?

☐ 지금 몇시야?/몇시니?[jigeum myeotsiya/myeotsini]
What time is it?

☐ 이거/그거/저거 뭐야?/뭐니?[igeo/geugeo/jeogeo mwoya/mwoni]
What is this/that/that?

☐ 이거/그거/저거 뭐예요?[igeo/geugeo/jeogeo mwoyeyo]
What is this/that/that, Mr. ~?

☐ 이거/그거/저거 주세요.[igeo/geugeo/jeogeo juseyo]
Please give me this/that/that, Mr. ~.

☐ 저는 스미쓰라고 합니다.[jeoneun seumissrago hamnida]
I'm Smith, sir.

☐ 나는 스미쓰라고 해.[naneun seumissrago hae]
I'm Smith.

☐ 선생님, 저의 이름은 에드워드 존입니다.
[seonsaengnim, jeoeui ireumeun Edward Johnimnida]
My name is John Edward, ma'am.

☐ 가자.[gaja]
Let's go.

☐ 갑시다.[gapsida]
Let's go, sir.

☐ 가지 마.[gaji ma]
Don't go.

☐ 할아버지, 가지 마세요.[harabeoji gaji maseyo]
Don't go, grandpa.

- [ ] **빨리 가자.** [bbali gaja]
Let's go quickly.

- [ ] **빨리 빨리 해.** [bbali bbali hae]
Do it quick, quick.

- [ ] **어서 오세요.** [eoseo oseyo]
Welcome, Mr. ~.

- [ ] **실례합니다.** [silyehamnida]
Excuse me, sir.

- [ ] **괜찮아?/괜찮니?** [gwaenchana/gwaenchanni)]
Is it OK?

- [ ] **괜찮다./괜찮아.** [gwaenchanta(gwaenchana)]
It's OK.(Fine.)

- [ ] **엄마, 괜찮아요?(=괜찮으세요?)** [eomma, gwaenchanayo(gwaenchaneuseyo)]
Mom, are you okay?

- [ ] **괜찮습니까?** [gwaenchanseumnikka]
Are you okay, sir?

- [ ] **사장님, 괜찮으십니까?** [sajangnim, gwaenchanseumnikka]
President, are you okay, sir?

- [ ] **괜찮습니다.** [gwaenchansseumnida]
It' OK, sir.

- [ ] **잘 먹겠습니다.** [jal meokkkesseumnida]
Thank you for this food, sir.

SECTION

04

문장의 구성

Structure of Sentence

In this section, we will learn about 5 formulas of sentence which are based on the elements for structure of sentence and about 품사(parts of speech).

1. Elements for structure of sentence

1 Signs of elements

Element	Sign	한국어
Subject	S	주어
Predicate	P	서술어
Complement	C	보어
Object	O	목적어
Adverbial word	AW	부사어
Postposition	PP	조사
Modifier	M	수식어
Independent word	IW	독립어

2 품사 and function in sentence

품사	Function in sentence
Noun(명사) Pronoun(대명사) Numeral(수사)	Indeclinable word(체언)
Postposition: PP(조사)	Connective word(관계언)
Verb(동사) Adjective(형용사)	Declinable word(용언)
Pre-noun(관형사) Adverb(부사)	Modifying word(수식언)
Exclamation(감탄사)	Independent word(독립언)

3 Rules for structure of sentence

① 주어, 보어, 목적어 and 부사어 consist of 체언(대명사, 명사, 수사) and 조사.

② 서술어 uses 용언(동사, 형용사) and 체언+서술격조사, of which the word-ending(어미) is inflected for the expression of tense, honorific, mood, etc.

③ 조사 is classified as follows. → Section 15

- PP for case(격조사)
  - Subjective PP(주격조사)
  - Objective PP(목적격조사)
  - Complementary PP(보격조사)
  - Pre-nominal PP(관형격조사)
  - Adverbial PP(부사격조사)
  - Predicative PP(서술격조사)
  - Vocative PP(호격조사)
- Auxiliary PP(보조사)

* 보조사 is used in stead of or together with 격조사 in the sentence.

* 관형격조사 can be said as 소유격조사(Genitive/Possessive PP).

④ 수식어 is divided as follows.

- 관형사 → Section 13
  - Numeral pre-noun(수관형사)
  - Demonstrative pre-noun(지시관형사)
  - Genitive pre-noun(소유격 관형사)
  - Specifying pre-noun(성상관형사)
    - Pure pre-noun(순수관형사)
    - Verbal pre-noun(동사적 관형사)
    - Adjectival pre-noun(형용사적 관형사)
- 부사 → Section 18
  - 성분부사(Adverb as an element of a sentence)
  - 문장부사(Adverb for the whole sentence)

⑤ 독립어 has no relation with other words in the a sentence and the types are 감탄사, conjunctive adverb and vocative case.

Note

* There is only "~의" in 관형격조사.

* There is only "~이다" in 서술격조사.

* 소유격 관형사 consists of 체언 and 관형격조사(~의).

* 형용사적 관형사 corresponds to the limiting adjective in English.

* 형용사 corresponds to the predicative adjective in English.

2. Five formulas of sentence

1 Formula 1: S(주어) + P(서술어)

① 영수(S)는 달린다(P)./영수가 달린다(←달리다).
Yeongsu runs./Yeongsu is the person who runs.

* "달리다(run)" is called as the dictionary form or basic form for 동사.

② 하늘은 푸르다.
The sky is blue.

③ 이것은 연필이다./이것이 연필이다.
This is a pencil./This is the thing that is a pencil.

④ 저것은 지우개(이)다./저것이 지우개다.
That is an eraser./That is the thing which is an eraser.

⑤ 이 집은 크다./이 집이 크다.
This house is big./This is the house which is big.

* "~가/이" is 주격조사 which focuses on 주어 and "~은/는" is 보조사 which focuses on 서술어. → Section 15
* 서술격조사(~이다) in ③ and ④ can be abbreviated as "~다.", when the last 음절 of 체언 has no 받침자음.
* "~가" and "~는" are used when the last 음절 of 주어(체언) has no 받침자음, "~이" and "~은" are used when there is 받침자음.
* "이" in ⑤ means "This" as 지시관형사.
* 서술어 in Formula 1 uses the complete intransitive verb(완전지동사), 형용사 or 체언+서술격조사.

2 Formula 2: S(주어) + C(보어) + P(서술어)

① 그녀(S)는 영희(C)가 아니다(P).
She is not Yeonghi.

② 너는 성인이 된다.
You become an adult.

③ 구름이 비가 된다.
The cloud becomes rain.

④ 이것은 옷이 아니다.
This is not clothes.

⑤ 코끼리는 코가 길다.
The nose of elephant is long.

* 보어 makes up for 주어 as a subjective complement(주격보어).
* "~가, ~이, ~은, ~는" which are used in Formula 1 as 주격조사 or 보조사 are also used for 보격조사 in Formula 2.
* 서술어 in Formula 2 uses incomplete intransitive verb(불완전자동사), 형용사 or negative 서술격조사(~이/가 아니다).

3 Formula 3: S(주어) + AW(부사어) + P(서술어)

① 이것(S)은 그것과 다르다(P).
This is different from that.

② 철수가 영수와 싸운다.
Cheolsu quarrels with Yeongsu.

③ 준기는 학교에 간다.
Jun-ki goes to school.

④ 학생은 선생님에게 인사한다.
The student salutes the teacher.

* "~과", "~와", "~에" and "~에게" are 부사격조사.
* "~과" and "~와" have the same meaning, but if there is no 받침자음 in the last 음절 of 체언, "~와" is used, and if there is 받침자음, "~과" is used.
* 부사어 makes up for 서술어.
* 서술어 in Formula 3 uses 불완전자동사 or 형용사.

4 Formula 4: S(주어) + O(목적어) + P(서술어)

① 나(S)는 빵(O)을 먹는다(P)./내가 빵을 먹는다.
I eat bread./I'm the person who eats bread.

② 아이는 공을 찬다./아이가 공을 찬다.
A child kicks ball./A child is the person who kicks ball.

③ 그는 축구를 좋아한다.
He likes football.

④ 순희는 화장품을 산다./순희가 화장품을 산다.
Sunhi buys cosmetics./The person who buys cosmetics is Sunhi.

* 목적격조사 are "~을" and "~를" only.
* "~를" is used when the last 음절 of 목적어 has no 받침자음 and "~을" is used when there is 받침자음.
* 서술어 uses the complete transitive verb(완전타동사).

5 Formula 5: S(주어) + AW(부사어) + O(목적어) + P(서술어)

① 나(S)는 철희에게(AW) 선물(O)을 준다(P).
I give a present to Cheolhi.

② 아버지(S)가 돈(O)을 아들에게(AW) 보낸다(P).
The father sends money to son.

③ 그 학생은 친구에게 편지를 쓴다.
That student writes a letter to friend.

④ 그는 목수에게 집을 짓게 한다.
He has a carpenter build a house.

* 서술어 in Formula 5 uses the incomplete transitive verb(불완전타동사) which needs 목적어 and 부사어 together.
* If 서술어 is a pure dative verb as in the sentences of ① and ②, the position of 부사어 and 목적어 can be exchanged.
* "~에게" is called as a dative postposition(여격조사) which is included in the category of 부사격조사.
* "그" in ③ is 지시관형사 which means "That" and the "그" in ④ is 대명사 which means "He".
* ④ is a causative sentence(사동문 → Section 20) by using auxiliary verb(~게 하다. → Section 16, 20).

3. 독립어 (IW)

1 Exclamation(감탄사)

① 아이고! 배가 아파요.
Ouch! I have a pain in stomach, Miss ~.

② 어머! 언제 왔어요?
Oh my goodness! When did you come, Mrs.~.

* "어머!" is used by woman, and "어!" is by man.

③ 만세! 우리가 이겼다.
Hurrah! We won.

④ 젠장! 또 비가 온다.
Damm it! Raining again.

* "젠장!" is used by man.

⑤ 이런! 지갑에 돈이 없다.
My goodness! No money in wallet.

⑥ 와, 꽃이 정말 아름답다!
Wow, What a beautiful flower!

2 Conjunctive adverb(접속부사) → Section 18

① 비가 온다. 그러나 나는 학교에 간다.
It rains. But I go to school.

② 돈이 없다. 그래서 우리는 가난하다.
No money. Therefore we are poor.

3 Vocative case

1 Name + 호격조사(~아/야)

① 철수야, 밥 먹어라(←먹다).
Cheolsu, have a meal.

② 영순아, 가자(←가다).
Yeongsun, let's go.

* 호격조사(~아, ~야) to the given name for the case where there is no need to be respectful like a friend or a young child.

* "~야" is used when the last 음절 of the name has no 받침자음 and "~아" is used when there is 받침자음.

* "~어라" is a word-ending for verb used in imperative sentence, and "~자" is a word-ending for verb used in Let's-sentence. → Section 9

2 Personal position or rank + 호격조사(~님)

① 사장님, 이것 잠깐 봐(← 보아 ← 보다/see, look at) 주십시오.
President! Please see this one for a minute, sir.

② 팀장님!
Boss, sir!

③ 기사님!
Driver, sir!

④ 장군님!
General, sir!

* "~님" is a honorific 호격조사 which implies high respect.

3 Name + Incomplete Noun(의존명사) → Section 14

① 영자 씨, 당신을 사랑해요.
Yeongja, I love you.

② 이희태 씨, / 희태 씨, 어디 계십니까?
Mr. Hitae Lee, / Hitae, Where are you, sir?

* "~ 씨" means Mr. ~, Miss ~ or Mrs. ~ to the full name or given name with respect.

③ 박현철 님, 이쪽으로 오십시오.
Mr. Hyeoncheol Park, please come here, sir.

* "~ 님" which is a honorific vocative 의존명사 to the full name with high respect.

* "오십시오." as a derivative of "오다(come)" is a high honorific imperative expression. → Section 8

④ 박영택 군, / 박 군, / 영택 군, 어떻게 지내는가?
Mr. Yeongtaek Park, / Mr. Park, / Yeongtaek, how are you?

* "~ 군" means Mr. which is used when the elder calls a young man formally.

⑤ 김희선 양, / 김 양, / 희선 양, 이것 좀 검토해 줘.
Miss Hiseon Kim, / Miss Kim, / Hiseon, please check this.

* "~ 양" means Miss. which is used when the elder calls an unmarried young woman formally.

SECTION

05

한글 쓰기 규칙

Rules for Writing Hangeul

1. Rules for spacing words (띄어쓰기 규칙)

Basically all words should be spaced, but there are exceptions as follows.

1 조사 should be written to the preceding word without space.

• 나는	I
• 나를	me
• 나의	my
• 나에게	to me
• 나처럼	like me

2 The incomplete noun(의존명사) → Section 14 of unit is usually spaced, but when the preceding word is Arabic number, 의존명사 should be written without space.

• 5000원(←오천 원)	5000₩(Won)
• 수박 10통(←열 통)	10 Watermelon
• 2019년 8월 15일 12시 30분	15. August 2019 12:30
• 말 20마리(←이십 마리)	20 horses

3 Nouns that express sequence, step, grade and the like can be written to the preceding word without space.

• 오 층/오층	the fifth floor
• 삼 학년/삼학년	grade three in school
• 두 시 삼십 분/두시 삼십분	two o'clock and half
• 제 삼 과/제삼과	the third Section

4 When monosyllabic word is written consecutively, these words can be written without space.

• 그 때/그때	that time
• 이 때/이때	this time
• 이 산과 저 산/이산과 저산	this mountain and that mountain
• 좀 더/좀더	some more

5 The order of Korean's full name is surname and then given name.

Mostly the full name is composed of one letter for surname and two letters for given name. But in the rare cases, it has two letters for surname and one or two letters for given name, or one letter for surname and one or three letters for given name.

Basically surname and given name should be written without space, but when it is necessary to clearly distinguish for the names of rare cases, it can be spaced.

- 홍길동
- 남궁동자/남궁 동자
- 선우진/선우 진
- 김구
- 박에리사

6 Special terminology can be written without space.

• 대륙간탄도탄 ← 대륙간 탄도탄	Intercontinental Ballastic Missile
• 골수성백혈병 ← 골수성 백혈병	Myeloid leukemia

2. Interceding "ㅅ[siot]": 사이시옷

사이시옷 is the name of "ㅅ" which is used to intercede the pronunciations between two words that are forming one compound noun(복합명사). In this case, 복합명사 is formed by two pure Korean words, or one pure Korean word and one Chinese origin, and there is no 받침자음 in the last 음절 of the preceding word.

1 The pronunciation of "ㅅ(t)" is added to the preceding word and the initial consonant of the first 음절 of the following word is pronounced strong as 경음.

• 부잣집[bujatjjip]	←	부자(rich man)+집(house)
• 귓병[guitbbyeong]	←	귀(ear)+병(disease)
• 햇볕[haetbbyeot]	←	해(sun)+볕(light)
• 나뭇가지[namutkkaji]	←	나무(tree)+가지(branch)
• 부둣가[budutkka]	←	부두(pier)+가(side)

* 부자(富者), 병(病) and 부두(埠頭) are Chinese origin.

2 The pronunciation of "ㄴ(n)" is added to the preceding word in front of the initial consonant("ㄴ" or "ㅁ") of the first 음절 of the following word.

• 잣눈[jannun]	←	자(ruler)+눈(scale)
• 빗물[binmul]	←	비(rain)+물(water)
• 존댓말[jondaenmal]	←	존대(treatment with respect)+말(word, speech)
• 본딧말[bondinmal]	←	본디(originality, the first)+말(word)

* 존대(尊待) is Chinese origin.

3 The pronunciation of "ㄴ(n)" is added to the preceding word in front of 중간모음 of the first 음절 of the following word and the pronunciation of 중간모음 changes to "ㄴ(n)";

- 깻잎[kkaennip] ← 깨(sesame)+잎(leaf)
- 나뭇잎[namunnip] ← 나무(tree)+잎(leaf)
- 뒷일[duinnil] ← 뒤(future)+일(affair)

- These following 복합명사 are abnormal cases because both of words are Chinese origin.

- 숫자[sutjja] ← 수(數)+자(字): number
- 곳간[gotkkan] ← 고(庫)+간(間): storeroom
- 셋방[setbbang] ← 세(貰)+방(房): room for rent
- 횟수[hoitssu] ← 회(回)+수(數): number of times, frequency
- 찻간[chatkkan] ← 차(車)+간(間): inside of train or car

3. Rules for writing words of foreign origin in 한글

1 The pronunciation of "ㅑ, ㅕ, ㅛ, ㅠ" should be written "ㅏ, ㅓ, ㅗ, ㅜ" as much as possible.

- Messiah[메싸이야] → 메시아
- television[텔레비젼] → 텔레비전
- version[버-젼] → 버전
- juice[쥬-쓰] → 주스
- laser[레이져] → 레이저
- chocolate[쵸-콜릳] → 초콜릿
- nature[네이쳐] → 네이처

2 The strong sound of "ㄲ, ㄸ, ㅃ, ㅆ, ㅉ" from the initial consonant should be written "ㅋ, ㅌ, ㅍ, ㅅ, ㅊ".

- Paris[빠리] → 파리
- café[까페] → 카페
- spy[쓰빠이] → 스파이

3 The pronunciation of long vowel is not indicated.

- juice[쥬-쓰] → 주스
- chocolate[쵸-콜릩] → 초콜릿
- New York[뉴- 요-ㅋ] → 뉴욕
- Tokyo[토-쿄-] → 도쿄
- book concert[부-ㅋ 콘서-트] → 북 콘서트

4 When the sound of "우" is pronounced faintly in the double vowel of "오우", "우" is deleted.

- boat[보우트] → 보트
- coat[코우트] → 코트
- rainbow[레인보우] → 레인보우

5 격음(aspirate sound) of "ㅋ, ㅌ, ㅍ" from 받침자음 should be written "ㄱ, ㅅ, ㅂ".

- chocolate[쵸-콜릩] → 초콜릿
- New York[뉴우 요-ㅋ] → 뉴욕
- book concert[부-ㅋ 콘서-트] → 북 콘서트
- pop song[팦 송] → 팝송
- tablet[태블릩] → 태블릿

SECTION

06 대명사

Pronoun

1. Personal pronoun (인칭대명사)

	person (인칭)	영어	한국어	humble title	honorific title
singular (단수)	1st	I	나, 내	저, 제	
	2nd	you	너, 네, 자네		당신, 사장님, 선생님, 여사님
	3rd	he	그, 그 남자		그분
		she	그녀, 그 여자		그분
plural (복수)	1st	we	우리/우리들	저희/저희들	
	2nd	you	너희/너희들		당신들, 사장님들 선생님들, 여사님들
	3rd	they	그들, 그 사람들		그분들

* "~들" is the plural suffix.

* The true meaning of "사장" is a president of company, and the true meaning of "선생" is a teacher, but these titles are used when calling an unfamiliar person with respect.

* "여사" means "Madam".

* 우리들, 너희들, 저희들: The meaning of plural overlaps, but can be used equally with "우리", "너희" and "저희".

* 내, 제, 네: These pronouns are used as the subjective pronoun(주격대명사) when 조사 is "~가" as well as the genitive pronoun(소유격대명사) as 준말 of "나의, 저의, 너의".

* "당신" is used to be polite when calling a stranger who looks younger or has a lower rank than the person speaking, but is also used when a married couple calls each other politely, or even when an argument occurs, to call the person spoken disparagingly, so it is necessary to be careful.

- 당신은 누구세요?/Who are you?
- 여보, 당신에게 미안해요./Honey, I feel sorry for you.
- 당신이 왜 우리 일에 참견해?/Why are you meddling in our business?

☐ 나는 너를 사랑한다./내가 너를 사랑한다.
I love you./I am the person who loves you.

☐ 저것은 내 책이다./저것이 내 책이다.
That is my book./That is the book which is mine.

☐ 그는 학생이다./그가 학생이다.
He is a student./He is the person who is a student.

☐ 그들(그 사람들)은 경찰이다./그들(그 사람들)이 경찰이다.
They are police./They are the people who are police.

☐ 너는 그녀를 좋아한다./네가 그녀를 좋아한다.
You like her./You are the man who likes her.

☐ 우리는/우리들은 행복하다.
We are happy.

☐ 저는 군인입니다./제가 군인입니다.
I'm a soldier, sir./I'm the man who is a soldier, sir.

"것" is an incomplete noun. → Section 14

☐ 그것은 제 모자입니다./그 모자는 제 것입니다.
That is my hat, madam./That hat is mine, madam.

☐ 저희는/저희들은 영어를 공부합니다.
We study English, sir.

☐ 그들은 테니스를 한다.
They play tennis.

☐ 너희는/너희들은 부지런하다.
You are diligent.

2. Demonstrative pronoun (지시대명사)

	this/here (near to the person speaking)	that/there (near to the person spoken)	that/there (away from the both)	Indefinite pronoun (부정대명사)
person	이이, 이분	그, 그이, 그녀, 그분	저이, 저분	아무(누구)
thing	이것	그것	저것	아무 것
place	여기, 이곳	거기, 그곳	저기, 저곳	아무 곳(데)
direction	이쪽	그쪽	저쪽	아무 쪽

* "것, 곳, 데, 분" are 의존명사. → Section 14

1 Example sentences

- 이이는 저의 남편입니다.
  This is my husband, madam.
- 이분은 교장선생님입니다.
  This is the principal of school, sir.
- 거기에 아무도/누구도 없다.
  There is nobody.
- 아무나/누구나 오너라.
  Come on anybody.
- 이것은 나의(=내) 책이다./이것이 나의(=내) 책이다.
  (=나의/내 책은 이것이다.)
  This is my book./This is the book which is mine.
  (=My book is this.)
- 그것은 너의(=네) 우산이다./그것이 너의(=네) 우산이다.
  (=너의/네 우산은 그것이다.)
  That is your umbrella./That is the umbrella which is yours.
  (=Your umbrella is that.)

- [ ] 아무 것이나 입어라.
Wear anything(any clothes).

- [ ] 여기는(이곳은) 그분의 집이다.
This place is his house.

- [ ] 저곳은(저기는) 극장이다.
That place is a theater.

- [ ] 아무 데라도(곳이라도) 가거라.
Go away anywhere.

- [ ] 아무(누구)도 여기로 들어갈 수 없습니다.
Nobody can enter here, sir.

- [ ] 영국 대사관은 이쪽이다.
This direction is toward the British Embassy.

* "~도", "~(이)나", "~(이)라도" are kinds of 보조사 → Section 15 which add additional meaning instead of 격조사.

* "~에", "~(에)서", "~(으)로" are 부사격조사. → Section 15

* "이이, 그이, 저이" are 인칭대명사 that a woman uses when referring her husband to others.

Note

In 한국어, the genitive pronoun(소유격 대명사) consists of 대명사 and 관형격조사(~의). (나의/mine, 너의/your, 그의/his, 그녀의/her, 그것의/its, 저것의/its, 우리의/our, 너희의/your, 그들의/their)

2 Demonstrative modifier(이, 그, 저, 아무) for pointing

1 When pointing at chair;

• 이 의자(들)	this chair(these chairs)
• 그 의자(들)	that chair(those chairs)
• 저 의자(들)	that chair(those chairs)
• 아무 의자(들)	any chair(any chairs)

2 When pointing at person;

• 이 사람(들)	this man(these people)
• 그 사람(들)	that man(those people)
• 저 사람(들)	that man(those people)
• 아무 사람(들)	anyone(any people)

3 When pointing at student;

• 이 학생(들)	this student(these students)
• 그 학생(들)	that student(those students)
• 저 학생(들	that student(those students)
• 아무 학생(들)	any student(any students)

SECTION

07

용언과 서술격조사의 시제

Tense of 용언 and 서술격조사

In 한국어, the structure of 용언 and 서술격조사 consists of a word-stem(어간) and a word-ending(어미). The conjugation for tense is implemented by inflexion of 어미. In this section the tense will be explained by example words based on the infinitive form.
The term of infinitive(부정사) only for 동사 in 영어 is applied to 동사, 형용사 and 서술격조사 in 한국어 because 형용사 and 서술격조사 are also conjugated for tense like 동사.

1. Common features of 용언 and 서술격조사

1 All of 부정사 have “~다” as 어미.

2 부정사 of 형용사 and 서술격조사 implies 현재시제.

3 For 현재시제 of 동사, “~ㄴ(받침자음)” or “~는~” is inserted between 어간 and 어미.

4 For 과거시제 of all, “~ㅆ(받침자음)”, “~았~” or “~었~” is inserted between 어간 and 어미.

5 For 대과거시제 of all, “~었~” is inserted additionally in front of 어미 of 과거시제.

6 For 미래시제, 어미 changes to “~ㄹ 것이다” or “~겠~” is inserted between 어간 and 어미.

Grammatical terms

- 시제: tense
- 현재시제: present tense
- 과거시제: past tense
- 대과거시제: past perfect tense
- 미래시제: future tense
  - 단순미래: simple future
  - 의지미래: volitional future
- 어간: word-stem(Unchanging part in the conjugation)
- 어미: word-ending(Changing part in the conjugation)
- 부정사: infinitive(Basic or dictionary form of 용언 and 서술격조사)

2. Conjugation of 용언 and 서술격조사

1 Conjugation according to each tense

	부정사 (어간+어미)	뜻	현재시제	과거시제	대과거시제	미래시제
서술격 조사	~(이)다	-	~이다./ ~다.	~이었다./ ~였다.	~이었었다./ ~였었다.	~일 것이다./ ~이겠다.
동사	가다 (가+다)	go	간다.	갔다.	갔었다.	갈 것이다/ 가겠다.
	오다 (오+다)	come	온다.	왔다.	왔었다.	올 것이다/ 오겠다.
	먹다 (먹+다)	eat	먹는다.	먹었다.	먹었었다.	먹을 것이다/ 먹겠다.
	사다 (사+다)	buy	산다.	샀다.	샀었다.	살 것이다/ 사겠다.
	팔다 (팔+다)	sell	판다.	팔았다	팔았었다.	팔 것이다/ 팔겠다.
	만나다 (만나+다)	meet	만난다.	만났다.	만났었다.	만날 것이다/ 만나겠다.
	배우다 (배우+다)	learn	배운다.	배웠다.	배웠었다.	배울 것이다/ 배우겠다.
	일하다 (일하+다)	work	일한다.	일했 (←하였)다.	일했 (←하였)었다.	일할 것이다/ 일하겠다.
	공부하다 (공부하+다)	study	공부한다.	공부했 (←하였)다.	공부했 (←하였)었다.	공부할 것이다/ 공부하겠다.
형용사	아름답다 (아름답+다)	beauti -ful	아름답다.	아름다웠다.	아름다웠었다.	아름다울 것이다./ 아름답겠다.
	빠르다 (빠르+다)	fast	빠르다.	빨랐다.	빨랐었다.	빠를 것이다./ 빠르겠다.
	덥다 (덥+다)	hot	덥다.	더웠다.	더웠었다.	더울 것이다/ 덥겠다.
	게으르다 (게으르+다)	lazy	게으르다.	게을렀다.	게을렀었다.	게으를 것이다./ 게으르겠다.

형용사	부지런하다 (부지런하+다)	diligent	부지런하다.	부지런했 (←하였)다.	부지런했 (←하였)었다.	부지런할 것이다./ 부지런하겠다.
	건강하다 (건강하+다)	healthy	건강하다.	건강했 (←하였)다.	건강했 (←하였)었다.	건강할 것이다./ 건강하겠다.
	시원하다 (시원하+다)	cool	시원하다.	시원했 (←하였)다.	시원했 (←하였)었다.	시원할 것이다/ 시원하겠다.
	있다 (있+다)	there is ~	있다.	있었다.	있었었다.	있을 것이다/ 있겠다.
	없다 (없+다)	there is no ~	있다.	없었다.	없었었다.	없을 것이다/ 없겠다.

* "~았~", "~었~" and "~겠~" which are added for tense are called as the preceding 어미(선어말어미) and "~다." is called as the final 어미(어말어미).

* In 과거시제, "~았~" is used when 모음 of the preceding 음절 is positive and "~었~" is used when 모음 is negative or neutral. However in case of irregular 용언, there are cases where this rule does not apply.

• ~이다 → ~이었다	• 가다 → 갔다(←가았다)
• 먹다 → 먹었다	• 오다 → 왔다(←오았다)
• 팔다 → 팔았다	• 만나다 → 만났다(←만나았다)
• 사다 → 샀다(←사았다)	• 배우다 → 배웠다(←배우었다)
• 있다 → 있었다	• 없다 → 없었다
• 웃다/laugh → 웃었다	• 차다/kick→찼다(←차았다)

* "~했다./~했었다." from "~하다" is 준말 of "~하였다./~하였었다".

* 용언 such as "가다", "오다", "일하다", "공부하다" and all 형용사 except "있다" and "없다" among the example words is called as irregular 용언(불규칙용언 → Section 16, 17).

* 용언 such as "먹다", "사다", "팔다", "배우다", "만나다", "있다" and "없다" is called as regular 용언(규칙용언).

* 대과거시제 indicates that the past state is no more in the present or is disconnected from the present.

* "~겠~" for 미래시제 implies the volition or the guess of the person speaking. The former is called as the volitional future(의지미래), the latter is called the simple future(단순미래).

* "~ㄹ 것이다." implies 단순미래.

* "~겠~" for 형용사 and 서술격조사 implies 단순미래 only. In case of 동사, only when the person speaking is the 1st person(I, we), "~겠~" implies 의지미래.

2 Example sentences

- [ ] 아버지는 컴퓨터를 ①판다./②팔았다./③팔 것이다.
  ① Father sells computer.
  ② Father sold computer.
  ③ Father will sell computer.

- [ ] 철수는 병원에 ①갔다./②갔었다./③갈 것이다.
  ① Cheolsu went to hospital.
  ② Cheolsu had gone to the hospital.
  ③ Cheolsu will go to the hospital.

- [ ] 어제 친구가 ①왔다./②왔었다.
  ① A friend came yesterday.
  ② A friend had come yesterday.

- [ ] 나는 내년에 운전을 ①배울 것이다./②배우겠다.
  ① I shall learn to drive next year.
  ② I will learn to drive next year.

- [ ] 영식이는 작년에 영어를 공부했었다.
  Yeonghsik had studied English last year.

- [ ] 어렸을 때, 그녀는 ①예뻤다./②예뻤었다.
  ① When young, she was beautiful.
  ② When young, she had been beautiful.

- [ ] 영식이는/영식이가 ①게으르다./②게을렀다.
  ① Yeongsik is lazy./Yeongsik is the person who is lazy.
  ② Yeongsik was lazy./Yeongsik is the person who was lazy.

  * "게으르다" is an irregular 형용사.

  * When the last 음절 of person's name has 받침자음, 주격조사 is "~이는/이가", but when there is no 받침 자음, 주격조사 is "~는/가". (영수는/영수가, 영철이는/영철이가, 영희는/영희가, 정숙이는/정숙이가)

☐ 그것은 미자의(하은이의) 모자였(←이었)다./우산이었다.
It was Mija's(Ha-eun's) hat/umblera.
* "~의" is 관형격조사 for possessive case.

3 Expression of guess of the person speaking for the present by using 부사 which implies 현재시제 by using 어미 for 미래시제

1 "(형용사)~ㄹ 것이다./~겠다."

☐ 필리핀은 지금 더울 것이다./덥겠다.
I guess that the Philippines is hot now.

☐ 한국은 아직 추울(←춥다/cold) 것이다./춥겠다.
I guess that Korea is still cold.

2 "(동사)~고 있을 것이다./~고 있겠다."

☐ 그는 지금 학교에 가고 있을 것이다./가고 있겠다.
I guess that he is on the way to school now.

☐ 철수는 오늘 공부하고 있을 것이다./있겠다.
I guess that Cheolsu is studying today.

3 (서술격조사)~일 것이다./~이겠다.

☐ 그 아이는 올해 여섯 살일 것이다./살이겠다.
The child will be six years old this year.

☐ 그녀는 지금 아마 수녀일 것이다./수녀이겠다.
I guess that she is probably a nun now.
* "아마" is 부사 that means 'perhaps, maybe, probably, likely, possibly'.

4 The progressive form of 동사

1 The present progressive form: (어간)~고 있다./~고 있는 중이다.

- [ ] 그는 지금 학교에 가고 있다./있는 중이다.
  He is on the way to school now.
- [ ] 나는 지금 영어를 공부하고 있다./있는 중이다.
  I'm studying English now.
- [ ] 그들은 사과를 먹고 있다./있는 중이다.
  They are eating apples.
- [ ] 명숙이는 운전을 배우고 있다./있는 중이다.
  Myeongsuk is learning to drive.

2 The past progressive form: (어간)~고 있었다./~고 있는 중이었다.

- [ ] 그는 학교에 가고 있었다./있는 중이었다.
  He was on the way to school.
- [ ] 나는 영어를 공부하고 있었다./있는 중이었다.
  I was studying English.
- [ ] 그들은 사과를 먹고 있었다./있는 중이었다.
  They were eating apples.
- [ ] 명숙이는 운전을 배우고 있었다./있는 중이었다.
  Myeongsuk was learning to drive.

3 The future progressive form: (어간)~고 있을 것이다./~고 있는 중일 것이다.

- [ ] 그는 학교에 가고 있을 것이다./~고 있는 중일 것이다.
  He will be on the way to school.
- [ ] 나는 영어를 공부하고 있을 것이다./~고 있는 중일 것이다.
  I shall be studying English.
- [ ] 그들은 사과를 먹고 있을 것이다./~고 있는 중일 것이다.
  They will be eating apples.
- [ ] 명숙이는 운전을 배우고 있을 것이다./~고 있는 중일 것이다.
  Myeongsuk will be learning to drive.

4 The past perfect progressive form: (어간)~고 있었었다./~고 있는 중이었었다.

"Please try by yourself, using the example sentences above."

* "~고 있는 중이다./중이었다./중일 것이다./중이었었다." emphasizes the progressive state more than "~고 있다./있었다./있을 것이다./있었었다.".

5 Usage of "~겠~"

1 When 주어 is the 1. person(I, we), "~겠~" to 동사 is for 의지미래.

- ☐ 우리는 오후에 그를 만나겠다(←만나다).
  We will meet him in the afternoon.
- ☐ 나는 저 집을 사겠다(←사다).
  I will buy that house.
- ☐ 내가 시장에 가겠다(←가다).
  I'm the person who will go to the market.

2 When 주어 is the 2nd, 3rd person or the thing, "~겠~" is used for the guess of the person speaking. In this case, "~ㄹ 것이다." or "~ㄹ 것 같다." can be used in stead of "~겠다.".

- ☐ 너는 학교에 늦겠다(←늦다)./늦을 것 같다./늦을 것이다.
  I guess that you will be late to school.
- ☐ 그는 이미 학교에 늦었겠다(←늦었다)./늦었을 것 같다./늦었을 것이다.
  I guess that he is already late to school.
- ☐ 기차가 택시보다 빠르겠다(←빠르다)./빠를 것 같다./빠를 것이다.
  I guess that the train will be faster than taxi.
- ☐ 철수는 이미 학교에 도착했겠다(←도착했다)./도착했을 것 같다./도착했을 것이다.
  I guess, Cheolsu has already arrived at school.

SECTION

08

낮춤표현과 높임표현

Non-honorific and Honorific Expression

The expression can be divided into 높임표현 using the honorific words(존댓말) and 낮춤표현 using the low forms of speech or the informal speaking(반말). And 높임표현 is redivided into three degrees which are colloquial, literary and high-honorific by inflecting 어미 of 용언 and 서술격조사. And then, the inflected 어미 for 높임표현 is reinflected according to the tense, the type of sentence and so on. In 한국어, 높임표현 is used even for the 3. person who is not together at the conversation.

1. 존댓말 and 반말

Refer to the list of 'Conjugation according to each tense' of Section 7.

1 If "요" is omitted, all of the colloquial 존댓말 changes to 반말 except 서술격조사(~이다). (가./가?, 와./와?, 먹어./먹어?, 사./사?, 팔아./팔아?, 공부해./공부해?, 아름다워./아름다워?...)

2 Dec.: Declarative, Int.: Interrogative

3 The honorific word of "먹다(eat)" is "들다(→ 드신다./드시냐? → 드세요./드세요? → 드십니다./드십니까?)".

반말		존댓말					
		colloquial[1]		literary		high–honorific	
Dec.[2]	Int.	Dec.	Int.	Dec.	Int.	Dec.	Int.
~(이)다.	~이냐?/ ~이야?	~이에요./ ~예요.	-?	~입니다.	-까?	~이십니다.	-까?
간다.	가느냐?/ 가?	가요.	〃	갑니다.	〃	가십니다.	〃
온다.	오느냐?/ 와?	와요.	〃	옵니다.	〃	오십니다.	〃
먹는다.	먹느냐?/ 먹어?	먹어요.	〃	먹습니다.	〃	드십니다.[3]	〃
산다.	사느냐?/ 사?	사요.	〃	삽니다.	〃	사십니다.	〃
판다.	파느냐?/ 팔아?	팔아요.	〃	팝니다.	〃	파십니다.	〃
만난다.	만나느냐?/ 만나?	만나요.	〃	만납니다.	〃	만나십니다.	“
배운다.	배우느냐?/ 배워?	배워요.	〃	배웁니다.	〃	배우십니다.	〃
일한다.	일하느냐?/ 일해?	일해요.	〃	일합니다.	〃	일하십니다.	〃
공부한다.	공부하느냐?/ 공부해?	공부해요.	〃	공부합니다.	〃	공부하십니다.	〃
아름답다.	아름다우냐?/ 아름다워?	아름다워요.	〃	아름답습니다.	〃	아름다우십니다.	〃
빠르다.	빠르냐?/ 빨라?	빨라요.	〃	빠릅니다.	〃	빠르십니다.	〃
덥다.	더우냐?/ 더워?	더워요.	〃	덥습니다.	〃	X	X
게으르다.	게으르냐?/ 게을러?	게을러요.	〃	게으릅니다.	〃	게으르십니다.	-까?

4 The honorific word of "있다(be, there is/are)" is "계시다(→ 계신다./계시냐? → 계세요./계세요? → 계십니다./계십니까?)".

5 "안" is 부사 which means "not".

부지런하다.	부지런하냐?/ 부지런해?	부지런해요.	〃	부지런합니다.	〃	부지런하십니다.	〃
건강하다.	건강하냐?/ 건강해?	건강해요.	〃	건강합니다.	〃	건강하십니다.	〃
시원하다.	시원하냐?/ 시원해?	시원해요.	〃	시원합니다.	〃	X	X
있다.	있느냐?/ 있어?	있어요.	〃	있습니다.	〃	계십니다.[4]	-까?
없다.	없느냐?/ 없어?	없어요.	〃	없습니다.	〃	안 계십니다.[5]	〃

Note

* To translate the literary or high-honorific 존댓말(~ㅂ니다, "~ㅂ니까? ~십니다, ~십니까?) which has no honorific title(경칭) into 영어 throughout this book, 경칭 is arbitrarily used among sir, madam, professor, boss or so on which expresses the respect for the stern or formal relationship.
* In case of colloquial 존댓말("~요.", "~요?" or "~요!"), 경칭 is arbitrarily used among grandpa, grandma, mammy, daddy, uncle, aunt, Mr. ~, Mrs. ~, Miss, ma'am or so on which expresses the respect for the friendly relationship.
* The interrogative 어미(~느냐?) is used mostly by old people. Instead of "~느냐?", "~ㄴ가?/~는가?" is also used by old people.
(가는가?, 오는가?, 파는가?, 공부하는가?, 아름다운가?, 있는가?, 없는가?...)

2. Rules for 존댓말 and 반말

1 High-honorific 존댓말 is more respectful than literary 존댓말 which is more respectful than colloquial 존댓말.

2 어미(~요) of colloquial 존댓말 is used really often and comfortably because it can imply declarative(~요.), interrogative(~요?), imperative(~요.), Let's(~요.) or exclamatory(~요!) for all of 5 types of sentence.→ Section 9

☐ 어디 가요?(⇗)
Where are you going, auntie?

☐ 시장에 가요.(⇘)
I'm going to the market, uncle.

☐ 빨리 와요.(⇒)
Come here quickly, Mr. ~.

☐ 아빠, 우리 놀러 가요.(⇘)
Let's go to play, daddy.

☐ 엄마, 꽃이 너무 예뻐요!(⇘)
What a beautiful flower, mommy!

* If the colloquial 존댓말 is used to the person spoken to whom you should keep the stern relationship like the unfamiliar and elder person, the director or manager in the company, the senior in the military, it can be a rude expression.

3 High-honorific 존댓말 is used for person and God only.

4 어미 of 존댓말(~요./~요?/~ㅂ니다./~ㅂ니까?) are used for the person spoken only.

5 어미 of high-honorific 존댓말(~십니다./~십니까?) are used for the person spoken only or for the 3. person together.

6 In case that the 3. person is younger or his position in workplace is lower than the person spoken, 존댓말 for the 3. person is not used.

3. Conjugation according to the tense

1 From the list of 'Conjugation on each tense' in Section 7:

1 When 어말어미(~다.) of 과거시제 is replaced with "~어./~어?", all changes to colloquial 반말, and when replaced with "~어요./~어요?", changes to colloquial 존댓말 like the following examples.

- ~이었다. → ~이었어./? → 이었어요./?
- ~였다. → 였어./? → 였어요./?
- 갔다. → 갔어./? → 갔어요./?
- 왔다. → 왔어./? → 왔어요./?
- 먹었다. → 먹었어./? → 먹었어요./?
- 건강했다. → 건강했어./? → 건강했어요./?

2 As the same way, the words of 대과거시제 change to colloquial 반말 and 존댓말 like the following examples.

- ~이었었다. → ~이었었어./? → ~이었었어요./?
- ~였었다.→~였었어./? → ~였었어요./?
- 갔었다. → 갔었어./? → 갔었어요./?
- 왔었다. → 왔었어./? → 왔었어요./?
- 먹었었다. → 먹었었어./? → 먹었었어요./?
- 건강했었다. → 건강했었어./? → 건강했어요./?

2 From the list of this Section 8:

1 When 어말어미(~요./~요?) of each of colloquial 존댓말 is replaced with "~ㅆ습니다./~ㅆ습니까?", all except 서술격조사 changes to literary 존댓말 of 과거시제 as the following examples.

- 가요./가요? → 갔습니다./갔습니까?
- 와요./와요? → 왔습니다./왔습니까?
- 먹어요./먹어요? → 먹었습니다./먹었습니까?
- 배워요./배워요? → 배웠습니다./배웠습니까?
- 건강해요./건강해요? → 건강했습니다./건강했습니까?
- ~입니다./입니까?(서술격조사) → ~이었습니다./~이었습니까?

2 For 대과거시제 of all literary 존댓말, "~었~" is inserted in front of "습니다./습니까?" of 과거시제.

- 갔습니다./갔습니까? → 갔었습니다./갔었습니까?
- 왔습니다./왔습니까? → 왔었습니다./왔었습니까?
- 먹었습니다./먹었습니까? → 먹었었습니다./먹었었습니까?
- 배웠습니다./배웠습니까? → 배웠었습니다./배웠었습니까?
- 건강했습니다./건강했습니까? → 건강했었습니다./건강했었습니까?
- ~이었습니다./~이었습니까? → ~이었었습니다./~이었었습니까?

3 과거시제 and 대과거시제 of high-honorific 존댓말

① For 과거시제, 어미 of "~십니다./~십니까?" changes to "~셨(←시었)습니다./~셨습니까?".

- 가십니다./가십니까? → 가셨습니다./가셨습니까?
- 오십니다./오십니까? → 오셨습니다./오셨습니까?
- 드십니다./드십니까? → 드셨습니다./드셨습니까?
- 배우십니다./배우십니까? → 배우셨습니다./배우셨습니까?
- 건강하십니다./건강하십니까? → 건강하셨습니다./건강하셨습니까?
- ~이십니다./~이십니까? → ~이셨습니다./~이셨습니까?

② For 대과거시제, "~었~" is inserted in front of "습니다./습니까?" of 과거시제 above.

- 가셨습니다./가셨습니까? → 가셨었습니다./가셨었습니까?
- 드셨습니다./드셨습니까? → 드셨었습니다./드셨었습니까?
- ~이셨습니다./~이셨습니까? → ~이셨었습니다./~이셨었습니까?

4. Example sentences using 존댓말 and 반말 case by case

1 반말 to the person spoken

- [ ] 너는 지금 어디 있느냐?/있어?
  Where are you now?

- [ ] 나는 이 시장에서 과일을 사./산다.
  I buy fruits in this market.

- [ ] 그는 매우 부지런해./부지런하다.
  He is very diligent.

- [ ] 나는 지금 학교에서 공부하고 있다./있어.
  Now I'm studying in the school.

- [ ] 순자는 교실에 없다./없어.
  Sunja is not in the classroom.

- [ ] 그 나라는 더워?/더우냐?
  Is that country hot?

- [ ] 철수는 열심히 공부하고 있어?
  Is Cheolsu studying hard?

  응, 열심히 공부하고 있어.
  Yes, studying hard.

  아니, 열심히 공부 안 해.
  No, not studying hard.

2 Colloquial or literary 존댓말 to the person spoken

□ 아저씨, 저는 친구 집에 가요.
I go to my friend's house, uncle.

□ 할아버지, 어디 가세요?
Grandpa, where are you going?

＊ "~세요." is also 어미 for colloquial 존댓말.

- 오다 → 오세요./오세요?
- 먹다(들다)→드세요./드세요?
- 있다(계시다)→계세요./계세요?
- 공부하다→공부하세요./공부하세요?

□ 엄마, 오늘 영수가 우리 집에 와요.
Mommy, today Yeongsu will come to our house.

□ 저의 형은 공장에서 일합니다.
My brother is working in the factory, sir.

□ 기택이는 창고에서 일하고 있습니다.
Gitaek is working in warehouse, sir.

□ 순자는 집에 없어요.
Sunja is not at home, Mrs. ~.

□ 비행기는 기차보다 더 빠릅니까?
Is the airplane faster than the train, sir?

예, 더 빠릅니다.
Yes, sir. Faster.

아니요. 더 느려요.
No, Mr. ~. Slower.

＊ "보다" is 부사격조사 which means "than". → Section 15

＊ "더" is 부사 which modifies the following 형용사, 관형사 or 부사 as the comparative.

3 High-honorific 존댓말 to the person spoken

- [ ] 선생님, 어디 가십니까?
  Sir, where are you going?

- [ ] 안녕히 주무십시오(←주무시다)./안녕히 주무셨습니까?
  Good night, madam!/Did you sleep well, madam?
  * "주무시다" is an honorific word of "자다(sleep)".

- [ ] 테니스를 매우 잘 치십니다(←치다).
  You are playing tennis very well, sir.

4 High-honorific 존댓말 to the 3. person and literary 존댓말 to the person spoken

- [ ] 오늘 저의 선생님이 우리 집에 오십니다.
  Today my teacher comes to our house, sir.

- [ ] 저의 어머니는 집에 계십니다.
  My mother is at home, madam.

- [ ] 교장선생님은 학교에 안 계십니다.
  The principal is not in the school, sir.

- [ ] 저의 아버지는 지금 농장에서 일하고 계십니다.
  My father is working in the farm now, sir.

- [ ] 저 할아버지는 정말 부지런하십니다.
  That grandfather is really diligent, sir.

- [ ] 사장님은 지금 사무실에 계십니까?
  Is the president in the office now, sir?

  예, 계십니다.
  Yes, sir. He is.

  아니요. 안 계십니다.
  No, sir. He is not.

5 High-honorific 존댓말 to the 3. person and 반말 to the person spoken

* "~십니다." changes to 반말 as follows.

- (동사)~십니다.: ~신다./~시냐?, ~셔./~셔?
- (형용사)~십니다.: ~시다.'시냐?, ~셔./~셔?
- (서술격조사)~이십니다.: ~이시다./~이시냐?, ~이셔./~이셔?

☐ 나의 선생님이 우리 집에 오신다./오셔.
My teacher comes to our house today.

☐ 나의 어머니는 집에 계신다./계셔.
My mother is at home.

☐ 저분이 우리 학교 교장선생님이시다./이셔.
That person is the principal of our school.

☐ 저 할아버지는 정말 부지런하시다./부지런하셔.
That grandfather is really diligent.

☐ 사장님은 지금 사무실에 계시냐?/계셔?
Is the president in the office now?

응, 계셔.
Yes. He is.

아니, 안 계셔.
No. He is not.

5. Proper honorific 용언

honorific	normal	현재시제	과거시제	미래시제
들다	먹다(eat) 마시다(drink)	드신다.	드셨다.	드실 것이다. 드시겠다.
드리다*	주다(give)	드린다.	드렸다.	드릴 것이다 드리겠다.
주무시다	자다(sleep)	주무신다.	주무셨다.	주무실 것이다. 주무시겠다.
편찮으시다	아프다(sick)	편찮으시다.	편찮으셨다.	편찮으실 것이다. 편찮으시겠다.
돌아가시다	죽다(die)	X	돌아가셨다.	돌아가실 것이다.
타계하시다	죽다(die)	X	타계하셨다.	타계하실 것이다
모시다*	안내하다(escort) 돌보다(take care)	모신다.	모셨다.	모실 것이다. 모시겠다.
계시다	있다(be, stay)	계신다.	계셨다.	계실 것이다. 계시겠다.
말씀하시다	말하다(say, tell)	말씀하신다.	말씀하셨다.	말씀하실 것이다 말씀하시겠다.
말씀드리다*	말하다(say, tell)	말씀드린다.	말씀드렸다.	말씀드릴 것이다. 말씀드리겠다.
뵈다*	보다(see) 만나다(meet)	뵌다.	뵈었다.	뵐 것이다. 뵙겠다.

Humble word(겸양어) is used for the person speaking to be humble and to express respect to the person spoken or the 3. person. And "~겠~" of 겸양어 is for 의지미래.

☐ 할아버지는 지금 방에서 주무시고 계십니다.
Grandpa is sleeping in the room, sir.

* "~고 계십니다." is a high-honorific 존댓말 of "~고 있습니다(←있다).".

☐ 할머니, 과일 드시겠어요?
Grandma, would you eat fruits?

☐ 나는 아버지를 모시고 학교에 갔다.
I escorted my father to the school.

* "~고" is a connective 어미 of 용언. → Section 21, 22

* "~에" is a 부사격조사 which implies direction to a place. → Section 15

* 모시고 가다: escort

☐ 어제 외할아버지가 돌아가셨습니다./타계하셨습니다.
My grandfather on mother's side died yesterday, sir.

☐ 나는 내일 선생님에게 이 책을 드리겠다.
I will give this book to the teacher tomorrow.

* "~에게" is 부사격조사 which implies the meaning of direction to the dative object with heart. In case of heartless object, "~에" is used.

나는 꽃밭에 물을 주었다.
I watered the flower garden.

나는 고양이에게 물을 주었다.
I gave the cat water.

☐ 사장님이 내일 오시겠다고 말씀하셨어요.
The president said that he would come tomorrow, Mr. ~.

* "~고" is 부사격조사 for indirect speech.

☐ 저는 내일 선생님을 뵙고 인사하겠습니다.
I will see the teacher tomorrow and greet him, sir.

SECTION

09 문장의 분류

Classification of Sentences

The sentences of 한국어 can be classified into five types which are based on 어미 of 서술어.

* 평서문: Declarative sentence
* 의문문: Interrogative sentence
* 명령문: Imperative sentence
* 청유문: Let's-sentence
* 감탄문: Exclamatory sentence

1. 평서문

평서문 transmits only the reality, truth, news, etc.

- ☐ 영수는 책을 읽는다.
  Yeongsu reads a book.

- ☐ 그 영화는 아주 재미있다.
  The movie is so interesting.

- ☐ 교수님, 저는 불어를 전공합니다.
  Professor, I major in French, sir.

- ☐ 할머니는 매우 건강하십니다.
  Grandma is very healthy, sir.

- ☐ 저는 한국말을 할 수 있습니다.
  I can speak Korean, sir.

- ☐ 어젯밤에 시내에서 화재가 발생했습니다.
  Last night a fire broke out in downtown, sir.

- ☐ 대한민국은 민주주의 국가이다.
  The Republic of Korea is a democratic country.

2. 의문문

의문문 is divided into yes/no(예/아니요) 의문문 which requires the answer with "Yes" or "No", and the interrogative(의문사) 의문문 which uses interrogative 대명사, interrogative 부사 or pre-noun(관형사) for interrogation.

1 예/아니요 의문문: The intonation goes up at the end of sentence.

☐ 밥 먹었어?(⇗)
Did you eat?

응/그래, 벌써 먹었어.(⇘)
Yes, I did already.

아니, 아직 안 먹었어.(⇘)
No, I did not yet.

☐ 저 영화 재미있어요?
Is that movie funny, Mr. ~.?

예, 재미있어요.
Yes, Mr. ~. It is funny.

아니요. 재미없어요.
No, Mr. ~. It is not funny.

☐ 공항은 가깝습니까?
Is the airport near, sir?

예, 가깝습니다.
Yes, sir. It is near.

아닙니다. 가깝지 않습니다.
No, sir. It is not near.

☐ 맛있게 드셨습니까?
Did you eat deliciously, sir?

예, 맛있게 먹었습니다.
Yes, sir. I ate deliciously.

아니요. 음식이 맛있지 않았습니다.
No, sir. The food wasn't delicious.

- Answer by "Yes" or "No"

	반말	존댓말
Yes	응./그래.	예.
No	아니.	아니요. * Colloquial
	아니야. * Stronger negation than "아니."	아닙니다. * Literary

2 의문사 의문문: At the end of sentence, the intonation goes down or goes up slightly.

누구/누	Who

- [ ] 너는 누구냐?(당신은 누구십니까?)
  Who are you(, sir)?
- [ ] 너는 누구에게 전화했느냐?
  Who did you call?
- [ ] 누가 너에게 전화했어?
  Who called you?

무엇, 뭐	What

* "이건" is abbreviation of "이것은". → Section 15

* "뭐" is abbreviation of "무엇" for colloquial expression.

- [ ] 이건 뭐야?(이것은 무엇이에요?)
  What is this(, Miss ~)?
- [ ] 지금 뭐하고 있어?(지금 무엇을 하고 계십니까?)
  What are you doing now(, sir?)

무슨	What

- [ ] 무슨 음식을 좋아해?
  What food do you like?
- [ ] 그것은 무슨 책이냐?
  What book is that?
- [ ] 무슨 생각을 하고 있어?
  What are you thinking?

어떤	What kind of

- [ ] 어떤 옷을 원하세요?
  What kind of clothes do you want, Mrs. ~?
- [ ] 그는 어떤 사람입니까?
  What kind of person is he, madam?

어느	Which

것
Incomplete noun
의존명사 → Section 14

- [ ] 어느 것이 너의 책이냐?
  Which is your book?
- [ ] 어느 차가 당신 것입니까?
  Which car is yours, sir?

몇	How many

- [ ] 하루에 몇 시간 일해요?
  How many hours a day do you work, Mr. ~?
- [ ] 한국에 몇 번 가셨(←시었)습니까.
  How many times have you been to Korea, sir?

몇째, 몇 번째	What number of

- [ ] 너는 몇째 아들이냐?
  What mnumber of son are you?
- [ ] 저는 둘째 아들입니다.
  I'm the second son, sir.

~로
부사격조사(→ Section 15)

- [ ] 그는 몇 번째로 도착했어?
  What is the number of his arrival?

언제	When

- [ ] 우리는 언제 출발해?
  When are we leaving?

것 같다
indicates a guess or an uncertain conclusion.

- [ ] 선생님, 한국은 언제 통일될 것 같습니까(←같다)?
  Sir, when do you think Korea will be unified?

어디	Where

~에, ~로
부사격조사

☐ 엄마, 제 모자는 어디에 있어요?
Where is my hat, mom?

☐ 철수야, 어디로 가느냐?
Where are you going, Cheolsu?

어떻게	How

☐ 그는 어떻게 학교에 갑니까?
How does he go to school, sir?

☐ 이 문제는 어떻게 풀어요?
How can I solve this problem, Mr. ~?

왜	Why

☐ 왜 영어를 공부해요?
Why do you study English, Mr. ~?

☐ 교수님, 한국은 왜 아직 통일을 못했습니까?
Why hasn't Korea been reunified yet, Professor?

얼마나	How ~

☐ 학교는 얼마나 멀어요?
How far is the school, Mr. ~?

☐ 기차로 얼마나 걸려요?
How long does it take by train, Mr. ~?

얼마	How much

☐ 이 신발은 얼마예요?
How much is this pair of shoes, Mr. ~?

☐ 이 시계는 얼마에 샀어?
How much did you pay for this watch?

☐ 월급은 얼마입니까?
How much is the salary, sir?

3 Interrogative 어미 of "~나요?" and "~ㄴ가요?"

These two 어미 are used customarily as colloquial 존댓말 with the intonation slightly down at the end of sentence.

1 (동사, 있다./없다.)~나요?

- ☐ 엄마, 우리는 언제 식사하나요?(=식사해요?)
  When do we eat, mommy?
- ☐ 그 소식을 믿어도 되나요?(=돼요?)
  Can I believe that news?
- ☐ 영수는 언제 오나요?(=와요?)
  When does Yeongsu come?
- ☐ 누가 교실에 있나요?(=있어요?)
  Who's in the classroom, ma'am?
- ☐ 해변에 사람이 없나요?(=없어요?)
  Is there nobody on the beach, Mr. ~?

2 [형용사, 서술격조사]~ㄴ가요?

- ☐ 선생님의 여자 친구는 예쁜가요?(=예뻐요?)
  Is the girlfriend of teacher pretty, Mr. ~?
- ☐ 그 일은 힘든가요?(=힘들어요?)
  Is that job difficult, Mr. ~?
- ☐ 영수는 학생인가요?(=학생이에요?)
  Is Youngsoo a student, Mrs. ~?
- ☐ 저 사람은 누구인가요?(=누구예요?)
  Who is that person, Mr. ~?

4 Interrogative 어미 of "~ㄹ까(요)?"

"~ㄹ까(요)?" is also colloquially used for guess of the person asking with the intonation slightly down at the end of sentence.

☐ 저 옷은 비쌀까(←비싸다)?
Do you think that those clothes are expensive?
/ Are those clothes expensive?

☐ 선생님의 여자 친구는 예쁠까요(←예쁘다)?
Do you think, the teacher's girlfriend is pretty, Mr. ~?
/ Is the teacher's girlfriend pretty, Mr. ~?

☐ 영수는 학생일까(←학생이다)?
Do you guess, Yeongsu is a student?
/ Is Yeongsu a student?

☐ 지금 교실에 학생들이 있을까요(←있다)?
Do you think, there are students in the classroom now, Mr. ~?

☐ 영수는 언제 도착할까요(←도착하다)?
When do you think, Yeongsu will arrive, Mr. ~?

☐ 내일 비가 올까(←오다)?
Do you guess, it will rain tomorrow?

5 Interrogative 어미 of "~(이)니?"

"~(이)니?" is also colloquially used often in 반말, which is more intimate than "~(ㄹ)까?", "~아/어?", "~느냐?" and "~는가/ㄴ가?". The intonation slightly drags and drops down at the end.

☐ 뭐 하니(←하다)?
What are you doing?

☐ 어디 가니(←가다)?
Where are you going?

☐ 오늘은 무슨 날이니(←날이다)?
What day is it today?

☐ 왜 늦었니(←늦다)?
Why are you late?

☐ 영수는 착하니(←착하다)?
Is Yeongsu good?

3. 명령문

명령문 has 6 types of the imperative 어미 of 동사 to the person spoken.

1 거라-불규칙동사(irregular verb)

2 너라-불규칙동사

5 "~아(~어)." is more strict than "~아(~어)라." like the military imperative style. "~게." is a friendly but formal expression that is used by the old to the young.

6 "~(으)세요." is friendly, but "~(으)시오." is formal and strict.

example (부정사)	뜻	존댓말			반말
		high –honorific ~(으)십시오.	colloquial ~(으)세요.[6]	literary ~(으)시오.[6]	~아(~어). /~아(~어)라. /~게.[5]
가다[1]	go	가십시오.	가세요.	가시오.	가./ 가거라./ 가게.
오다[2]	come	오십시오.	오세요.	오시오.	와./ 오너라./ 오게.
주다	give	주십시오.	주세요.	주시오.	줘./ 주어라./ 주게.
앉다	sit down	앉으십시오.	앉으세요.	앉으시오.	앉아./ 앉아라./ 앉게.
일어서다	stand up	일어서십시오.	일어서세요.	일어서시오.	일어서./ 일어서라./ 일어서게.
읽다	read	읽으십시오.	읽으세요.	읽으시오.	읽어./ 읽어라./ 읽게.
파다	dig	파십시오.	파세요.	파시오.	파./ 파라./ 파게.
하다[3]	do	하십시오.	하세요.	하시오.	해./ 해라./ 하게.
묻다	bury	묻으십시오.	묻으세요.	묻으시오.	묻어./ 묻어라./ 묻게.
엎드리다	prostrate oneself	엎드리십시오.	엎드리세요.	엎드리시오.	엎드려./ 엎드려라./ 엎드리게.

세우다	stand, erect	세우십시오.	세우세요.	세우시오.	세워./ 세워라./ 세우게.
방문하다[3]	visit	방문하십시오.	방문하세요.	방문하시오.	방문해. / 방문해라./ 방문하게.
질문하다[3]	ask a question	질문하십시오.	질문하세요.	질문하시오.	질문해./ 질문해라./ 질문하게.
보여 주다[4]	show to someone	보여 주십시오.	보여 주세요.	보여 주시오.	보여 줘./ 보여 주어라./ 보여 주게
읽어 주다[4]	read to someone	읽어 주십시오.	읽어 주세요.	읽어 주시오.	읽어 줘./ 읽어 주어라./ 읽어 주게.

3 여-불규칙동사(해←하여)

4 "~아/어 주다(serve)" is an auxiliary 동사(보조동사) which follows the main 동사.* 보조동사 and 불규칙 동사 → Section 16

- [ ] 여기 앉으세요.
  Please sit down here.

- [ ] 소파에 앉으십시오.
  Please sit down on the sofa, sir.

- [ ] 여권을 보여 주세요.
  Please show me the passport.

- [ ] 이리 와.
  Come here.

- [ ] 저리 가.
  Get out here./Go away.

- [ ] 잠깐만 기다리세요.
  Please wait a moment.

- [ ] 시원한 물 한 잔 주세요.
  Please give me a glass of cold water.

- [ ] 땅을 깊게 파라.
  Dig deep in the ground.

- [ ] 매일 성경을 읽어라.
  Read the bible everyday.

- [ ] 박 군, 이 일은 자네가 하게.
  Park, you do this job, please!

4. 청유문

청유문 is the sentence that the person speaking persuades the person spoken to do together. To emphasize the conviction of persuasion, "우리(we)", "함께(together)" or "같이(together)" can be used together.

Example (부정사)	반말	존댓말		
		colloquial	literary	high–honorific
	~자.	~(아)요./~(어)요.	~ㅂ시다.	~(으)십시다.
타다 (ride)	타자.	타요.	탑시다.	타십시다.
가다 (go)	가자.	가요.	갑시다.	가십시다.
걷다 (walk)	걷자.	걸어요.	걸읍시다.	걸으십시다.
일어나다 (get up)	일어나자.	일어나요.	일어납시다.	일어나십시다.
먹다 (eat)	먹자.	먹어요.	먹읍시다.	드십시다.
달리다 (run)	달리자.	달려요.	달립시다.	달리십시다.
버리다 (throw away)	버리자.	버려요.	버립시다.	버리십시다.
산책하다 (take a walk)	산책하자.	산책해요.	산책합시다.	산책하십시다.
웃다 (laugh)	웃자.	웃어요.	웃읍시다.	웃으십시다.

결혼하다 (marry)	결혼하자.	결혼해요.	결혼합시다.	X

☐ 우리 결혼하자.
Let us marry.

☐ 점심으로 삼계탕을 먹읍시다.
Let's eat Samgyetang for lunch, sir.

☐ 오후에 우리 산책하십시다.
Let us take a walk in the afternoon, sir.

☐ 그만 자고 일어나자.
Let's finish sleeping and get up.

☐ 저기까지 같이 달리자.
Let's run till there together.

☐ 함께 크게 웃어요.
Let's laugh loudly together, gentlemen.

☐ 우리 손잡고 걷자.
Let's walk hand in hand.

☐ 함께 택시를 타요.
Let's ride in a taxi together, Mr. ~.

5. 감탄문

감탄문 expresses emotional and physical feeling. To emphasize the feeling in 감탄문, the following 부사 are used together; "아주(quite), "무척(excessively)", "매우(very)", "정말(really)", "진짜(truly, really)", "굉장히(excellently)", "대단히(extremely)", "너무(too)", "참(truly)", "되게(exceedingly)".
The exclamation mark(!) is not always necessary , if the feeling is not so strong.

1 어미 for 감탄문

example (부정사)	반말				존댓말(colloquial)	
	~(는)구나!	~(는)군!	~네!	~아라!/어라!	~(는)군요!	~네요!
예쁘다, 아름답다 (beautiful)	예쁘구나! 아름답구나!	예쁘군! 아름답군!	예쁘네! 아름답네!	예뻐라! 아름다워라!	예쁘군요! 아름답군요!	예쁘네요! 아름답네요!
맛있다 (delicious)	맛있구나!	맛있군!	맛있네!	맛있어라!	맛있군요!	맛있네요!
어렵다 (difficult)	어렵구나!	어렵군!	어렵네!	어려워라!	어렵군요!	어렵네요!
(피아노를) 치다 [play (the piano)]	치는구나!	치는군!	치네!	X	치는군요!	치네요!
잘하다 (do well)	잘하는구나!	잘하는군!	잘하네!	X	잘한는군요!	잘하네요!
변하다 (change)	변하는구나!	변하는군!	변하네!	X	변하는군요!	변하네요!
고생하다 (suffer hardship)	고생하는 구나!	고생하는군!	고생하네!	X	고생하는 군요!	고생하네요!

* In case of 동사, "~(아)라!/~(어)라!" is not applicable.
* "~구나!" and "~군요!" are for 형용사 and 서술격조사.
* "~는구나!" and "~는군요!" are for 동사.
* 어미 of literary and high-honorific 존댓말(~ㅂ니다! and ~십니다!) can be used in 감탄문 with exclamation mark(!).

☐ 아이고, 어려워라!
Oh my! How difficult it is!

☐ 이 빵은 정말 맛있군요!
This bread is really delicious, Mr. ~!

☐ 네 딸은 무척 예쁘구나!
Your daughter is so pretty!

☐ 저 사람은 마음이 너무 쉽게 변하는군.
That person's mind changes too easily.

☐ 그 질문은 너무 어렵네요.
That question is too difficult, Mr. ~.

☐ 영수는 피아노를 아주 잘 치는구나!
Yeongsu plays the piano quite well!

☐ 저 분은 시장님이시군요./시장님이시네요.
That person is the mayor, Mr. ~.

잘
means 'well, nicely, exactly, carefully' as 부사.

☐ 한국말을 진짜 잘 하십니다./잘 하시네요!/잘 하시는군요!
Really you are fluent in Korean, madam. ~!

☐ 사업 때문에 무척 고생하십니다!/고생하시는군요!/고생하시네요.!
You are suffering a lot of hardship because of business, sir!

☐ 강 사장님, 영어가 매우 유창하십니다.!/유창하시군요!/유창하시네요!
President Kang, your English is very fluent, sir!

* "~시군요!/~시네요!" for 형용사/서술격조사 and "~시는군요!/~시네요!" for 동사 are used as high-honorific 존댓말 in 감탄문. (예쁘시군요!/예쁘시네요!, 치시는군요!/치시네요!.....)

2 감탄문 using 평서문

평서문 can be used as 감탄문 by adding the exclamatory word at the head of sentence together with 부사 for exclamation which are enumerated above.

- ☐ 와, 이 사과 정말 크다!
  Great! This apple is really big!

- ☐ 우와, 영숙이는 노래를 참 잘한다!
  Wow! Yeongsuk is singing really well!

- ☐ 어머, 정말 큰 일이에요!
  Oh my! Really big happening it is, Mrs. ~!

SECTION

10 부정문

Negative Sentence

1. Negative 서술격조사

The negative form of 서술격조사 is "~이/가 아니다".

☐ 이것은 집이다. → 이것은 집이 아니다.
This is a house. → This is not a house.

☐ 저것은 소나무다. → 저것은 소나무가 아니다.
That is a pine tree. → That is not a pine tree.

* If the last 음절 of 체언 has no 받침자음, the negative 서술격조사 is "~가 아니다.", and if there is 받침자음, it is "~이 아니다.".

The inflection of "아니다(not, no)." according to the degrees of 높임표현 for each tense is as follows.

어미 of "~야." expresses the firmer self-confidence than "~(이)다." in 반말.

* If there is no additional word which implies 미래시제 in sentence, these negative 서술격조사 expresses the guess in 현재시제.

Tense	반말	존댓말		
		colloquial	literary	high-honorific
현재시제	아니다./ 아니야.	아니에요.	아닙니다.	아니십니다.
과거시제	아니었다./ 아니었어.	아니었어요.	아니었습니다.	아니셨습니다.
미래시제*	아닐 것이다./ 아닐 것이야.	아닐 거예요.	아닐 것입니다.	아니실 것입니다.

☐ 저는 영호예요. → 저는 영호가 아니에요.
I'm Yeongho, uncle. → I'm not Yeongho, uncle.

☐ 저 학생은 영철이 아닙니까?
Is that student not Yeongcheol, sir?

예, 그는 영철이 아닙니다.
No, sir. He is not Yeongcheol.

아닙니다. 그는 영철입니다.
Yes, sir. He is Yeongcheol.

□ 그 학생은 박 영만이에요. → 그 학생은 박 영만이 아니에요.
That student is Yeongman Park, Mr. ~.
→ That student is not Yeongman Park, Mr. ~.

□ 저 사람은 경찰관이냐?
Is that person is a policeman?

응, 저 사람은 경찰관이야.
Yes. That person is a policeman.

아니, 그 사람은 경찰관이 아니야.
No. he is not a policeman.

□ 이것은 의자냐?
Is this a chair?

응, 그것은 의자야.
Yes. That is a chair.

아니, 그것은 의자가 아니야.
No. That is not a chair.

□ 저것은 책상입니까?
Is that a desk, sir?

아닙니다. 저것은 책상이 아닙니다.
No, sir. That is not a desk.

예, 저것은 책상입니다.
Yes, sir. That is a desk.

□ 저분은 시장님이시다. → 저분은 시장님이 아니시다.
That person is the mayor. → That person is not the mayor.

□ 저분은 회사 사장님이십니다. → 저분은 회사 사장님이 아니십니다.
That person is the president of a company, sir.
→ That person is not the resident of a company, sir.

□ 선생님은 의사십니까? → 선생님은 의사가 아니십니까?
Are you a doctor, sir? → Aren't you a doctor, sir?

□ 내일 그 학생이 가는(→ 가다) 곳은 도서관이 아닐 것이다.
The place where the student goes tomorrow will not be the library.

* "가는" which is derived from "가다(go)" is a verbal pre-noun.
→ Section 13

2. Negative 용언

부정문 using 용언 is divided into 안-부정문 and 못-부정문.

1 안-부정문

안-부정문 expresses the negative situation only and is redivided into Short 안-부정문 and Long 안-부정문 under the same meaning.

1 안-부정문 using 동사

☐ 나는 학교에 간다.
I go to school.

나는 학교에 안 간다.(Short 안-부정문 with 부사 of "안/not")

나는 학교에 가지 않는다.(Long 안-부정문 with 보조동사 of "~지 않다") → Section 16
I do not go to school.

* The inflection of "**않다**(do not)" according to the degrees of **높임표현** for each tense is as follows.

Tense	반말	존댓말		
		colloquial	literary	high-honorific
현재시제	않는다./않아.	않아요.	않습니다.	않으십니다.
과거시제	않았다./않았어.	않았어요.	않았습니다.	않으셨습니다.
미래시제*	않을 것이다./ 않을 것이야.	않을 거예요.	않을 것입니다.	않으실 것입니다.

* Refer to "아니다." of 미래시제.

☐ 너는 학교에 안 가?
Don't you go to school?

응, 안 가.
No, I don't go.

아니, 가.
Yes. I go.

☐ 저는 학교에 안 가요./저는 학교에 가지 않아요.
I do not go to school, Mr. ~.

☐ 나는 학교에 안 갈 것이다./나는 학교에 가지 않을 것이다.
I won't go to school.

- The Short 안-부정문 can not be applied to "~하다"-동사. (Example: 공부하다/study, 일하다/work)
  - 안 공부한다.(×) → 공부하지 않는다.(○)
  - 안 일했어요.(×) → 일하지 않았어요.(○)

2 안-부정문 using 형용사

☐ 오늘은 덥다.
It is hot today.

☐ 오늘은 안 덥다.(Short 안-부정문 with 부사 of "안")
오늘은 덥지 않다.(Long 안-부정문 with 보조형용사 of "~지 않다") → Section 17
It is not hot today.

☐ 아빠, 오늘은 안 더워요./오늘은 덥지 않아요.
It is not hot today, daddy.

☐ 어제는 안 더웠습니다./어제는 덥지 않았습니다.
It was not hot yesterday, sir.

☐ 내일은 안 더울 것이다./내일은 덥지 않을 것이다.
It will not be hot tomorrow.

* The inflection of "않다" as 보조형용사 is the same as 보조동사 above except 반말 in 현재시제(않는다./않아.→않다./않아.).

2 못-부정문

못-부정문 is also redivided into Short 못-부정문 and Long 못-부정문 under the same meaning.

① 못-부정문 using 동사 to express the inability for doing something.

□ **나는 수영을 못 한다.** (Short 못-부정문 with 부사 of "못/can not")

나는 수영을 하지 못한다. (Long 못-부정문 with 보조동사 of "~지 못하다")

I can not swim.

□ 저는 자전거를 못 탑니다./저는 자전거를 타지 못합니다.

I can not ride a bicycle, sir.

* The inflection of "못하다(can not do)" according to the degrees of **높임표현** for each tense is as follows.

Tense		존댓말		
		colloquial	literary	high-honorific
현재시제	못한다./못해.	못해요.	못합니다.	못하십니다.
과거시제	못했다./못했어.	못했어요.	못했습니다.	못하셨습니다.
미래시제*	못할 것이다./ 것이야.	못할 거예요.	못할 것입니다.	못하실 것입니다.

* Refer to "아니다." of 미래시제.

The Short 못-부정문 also can not be applied to "~하다"-동사 (Ex.: 노래하다/sing, 사용하다/use).

- 못 노래합니다.(×) → 노래하지 못합니다.(○)
- 못 사용할 거예요.(×) → 사용하지 못할 거예요.(○)

② 못-부정문 using 형용사 to express the deficiency in something

□ **그는 유능하지 못하다.**(Long 못-부정문 with 보조형용사 of "~지 못하다")

He is lacking in ability.

□ 물이 맑지 못했다.

The water was deficient in clearness.

* In case of 형용사, there is no short 못-부정문, and the inflection of "못하다" as 보조형용사 is the same as 보조동사 above except 반말 in 현재시제(못한다./못해.→못하다./못해.).

3. Negative 명령문(부정명령문) and negative 청유문(부정청유문)

To express the meaning of negation in 명령문 and 청유문, 보조동사 of "~지 말다" is used.

1 Inflection of "말다"

		부정명령문	부정청유문
반말		마./마라./말아라./말게.	말자.
존댓말	colloquial	마세요./말아요.	말아요.
	literary	마시오.	맙시다.
	high-honorific	마십시오.	마십시다.

2 Example sentences

1 부정명령문

- 수영장에 들어가지 마./마라./말아라./말게.
  Don't go into the pool!
- 여기서 담배를 피우지 마세요./마시오(More stern than "마세요.").
  Don't smoke here, gentlemen!
- 사무실에서 술을 마시지 마십시오.
  Don't drink alcohol in the office, sir!
- 밖으로 나가지 마.
  Don't go out!
- 여보, 눈물을 흘리지 말아요.
  Don't shed tears, darling!

"여보" is used by a married couple to call each other.

- For notice, "~금지(No/Forbidden)" is used.
  - 수영금지: Swimming forbidden
  - 흡연금지: No smoking
  - 외출금지: Leave forbidden
  - 소변금지: No urinating
  - 취사금지: No cooking
  - 쓰레기 무단투기 금지: No dumping waste without permission

2 부정청유문

☐ 서로 속이지 맙시다.
Don't let us fool each other, sir!

☐ 우리 싸우지 말자.
Let's not fight!

☐ 언쟁하지 마십시다.
Please, let's not argue, sir!

When "우리" is used as 주어 in 청유문, it emphasizes the camaraderie.

☐ 우리 이제부터 헤어지지 말아요.
Let's not break up from now on, dear!

SECTION

11 수사

Numeral

1. Cardinal number and Ordinal number (기수와 서수)

English (기수/서수)	Korean (기수/서수)	Chinese origin (기수/서수)
0	영	영
1/1st	하나/첫째(첫 번째)	일/제일
2/2nd	둘/둘째(두 번째)	이/제이
3/3rd	셋/셋째(세 번째)	삼/제삼
4/4th	넷/넷째(네 번째)	사/제사
5/5th	다섯/다섯째(다섯 번째)	오/제오
6/6th	여섯/여섯째(~ 번째)	육/제육
7/7th	일곱/일곱째(~ 번째)	칠/제칠
8/8th	여덟/여덟째(~ 번째)	팔/제팔
9/9th	아홉/아홉째(~ 번째)	구/제구
10/10th	열/열 번째	십/제십
11/11th	열하나/열한 번째	십일/제십일
12/12th	열둘/열두 번째	십이/제십이
13/13th	열셋/열세 번째	십삼/제십삼
14/14th	열넷/열네 번째	십사/제십사
19/19th	열아홉/열아홉 번째	십구/제십구
20/20th	스물/스무 번째	이십/제이십
21/21st	스물하나/스물한 번째	이십일/제이십일
30/30ht	서른/서른 번째	삼십/제삼십
40/40th	마흔/마흔 번째	사십/제사십
50/50th	쉰/쉰 번째	오십/제오십
60/60th	예순/예순 번째	육십/제육십
70/70th	일흔/일흔 번째	칠십/제칠십
80/80th	여든/여든 번째	팔십/제팔십

90/90th	아흔/아흔 번째	구십/제 구십
100/100th	백/백 번째	백/제 백
111/111th	백열하나/백열한 번째	백십일/제 백십일
1,000	천	천
10,000	만	만
100,000	십만	십만
1,000,000	백만	백만
10,000,000	천만	천만
100,000,000	일억	일억
1,000,000,000	십억	십억

2. Practical use of numbers

1 Signs of arithmetic calculations

- \+ 더하기(←더하다)
- \- 빼기(←빼다)
- × 곱하기(←곱하다)
- ÷ 나누기(←나누다)

"~(이)야." expresses emphasis or firm confidence in 반말.

☐ 칠 더하기 십일은 십팔입니다./십팔이에요./십팔이다./십팔이야.
7+11=18

☐ 십이 빼기 칠은 오입니다./오예요./오다./오야.
12-7=5

☐ 사 곱하기 삼은 십이예요.
4×3=12

☐ 십 나누기 오는 이다.
10÷5=2

2 Reading fractional number

• fractional number	분수
• denominator	분모
• numerator	분자

- 1/2: 이분의 일, 반
- 1/3: 삼분의 일
- 2/3: 삼분의 이
- 1/7: 칠분의 일
- 5/7: 칠분의 오
- 1/10: 십분의 일
- 4/10: 십분의 사
- 9/10: 십분의 구
- $1\frac{1}{2}$: 일과 이분의 일
- $2\frac{3}{4}$: 이와 사분의 삼
- $4\frac{3}{8}$: 사와 팔분의 삼
- $6\frac{7}{8}$: 육과 팔분의 칠

3 Reading decimal number

• decimal number	소수
• decimal	소수점

- 0.5: 영 점 오
- 8.25: 팔 점 이오
- 12.71: 십이 점 칠일
- 102.34: 백이 점 삼사

4 Reading year

• B.C. Yr. 235	기원전 이백삼십오 년
• A.D. Yr 537	서기 오백삼십칠 년
• Yr. 1987	천구백팔십칠 년
• Yr. 2019	이천십구 년

5 Reading long number

• 1,000,000,000	십억
• 10,000,000,000	백억
• 100,000,000,000	천억
• 1,000,000,000,000	일조

- 2,197,365 → 이백십구만 칠천삼백육십오
- 3,457,865,354 → 삼십사억 오천칠백팔십육만 오천삼백오십사
- 987,654,321,000 →구천팔백칠십육억 오천사백삼십이만 천
- 1,123,456,789,200 →일조 천이백삼십사억 오천육백칠십팔만 구천이백

* It reads four figures(oooo조oooo억oooo만oooo) separately as one group.

* There are no Korean cardinal and ordinal for 백, 천, 만...

3. Unit(단위) for counting

Unit	Relevant object	Example use
채	house	집 세 채(3 houses)
대	means of transportation, machine, etc	트럭 세 대(3 trucks) 자전거 두 대(2 bicycles) 비행기 다섯 대(5 airplanes) 피아노 한 대(1 piano), 세탁기 두 대(2 washing machines)
칸	room, office	방 네 칸(4 rooms) 사무실 두 칸(2 offices)
권	book	책 세 권(3 books) 잡지 여섯 권(6 magazines)
장	paper, glass, etc	종이 일곱 장(7 sheets of paper) 창문유리 여덟 장(8 panes of glass for window)
척	ship [1]	군함 아홉/구 척(9 warships) 화물선 열/십 척(10 cargo ships) 어선 열한/십일 척(11 fishing boats)

1 Korean and Chinese 기수 can be used together.

켤레	shoes, socks, gloves	운동화 열두 켤레(12 pairs of sports shoes) 양말 열세 켤레(13 pairs of socks) 장갑 열네 켤레(14 pairs of gloves)
평	size of house or lot (1 평=3.3 m²) 1	서른두/삼십이 평 아파트 (apartment of 32 Pyung) 논 이백 평(rice field of 200 Pyung) 산 오천 평(mountain of 5000 Pyung)
명	person 1	학생 열일곱/십칠 명(17 students) 어린이 쉰/오십 명(50 children) 군인 예순한/육십일 명(61 soldiers)
분	person ※ honorific word of "명"	국회의원 열 분(10 members of the National Assembly) 선생님 다섯 분(10 teachers)
마리	animal, fish, bird, insect, etc	말 열 마리(10 horses) 닭 두 마리(2 chickens) 잉어 세 마리(3 carps) 고래 네 마리(4 whales) 나비 다섯 마리(5 butterflies)
살	age	열일곱 살 소녀(17 year old girl) 이른 살 할아버지(70 year old grandpa)
세	age 2 ※ honorific word of "살"	백 세 노인(100 year old person)
근	weight ※1근=600g	생강 두 근(2 Geuns of ginger) 쇠고기 열 근(10 Geuns of beef)
병	bottle	맥주 세 병(3 bottles of beer)
잔	cup, glass	커피 한 잔(1 cup of coffee) 물 한 잔(1 glass of water)
공기	bowl of boiled rice	밥 두 공기(2 bowls of boiled rice)
포기	plant, seedling, (head of) vegetable	풀 한 포기(a single plant) 오이모종 두 포기(2 seedling of cucumber) 배추 세 포기(3 heads of white cabbage)
자루	tool with long handle or grip	연필 네 자루(4 pencils) 삽 다섯 자루(5 shovels) 도끼 여섯 자루(6 axes)
	sack	쌀 여덟 자루(8 sacks of rice) 감자 아홉 자루(9 sacks of potato)
그루	tree	소나무 열 그루(10 pine trees) 사과나무 스물두 그루(22 apple trees)

2 Only Chinese 기수 can be used.

송이	flower	장미 서른한 송이(31 roses) 국화 백한 송이(101 chrysanthemums)
	grape, banana, etc	포도 세 송이(3 bunches of grape) 바나나 열 송이(10 bunches of banana)
번	number of times	턱걸이 열두 번(12 times of pull-up) 여러 번(several times)
	numerical order [2]	사 번 타자(the 4th batter)
회	count times [2]	팔굽혀펴기 십 회(10 times of push-up)
다발	flower, hay, etc	꽃 한 다발(1 bundle of flowers) 건초 두 다발(2 bundles of hay) 장작 세 다발(3 bundles of firewood)
개	each separate thing	복숭아 세 개(3 peaches) 비누 세 개(3 pieces of soap) 캔디 열 개(10 pieces of candy)
끼	meal	식사 한 끼(1 meal)
벌	clothes	옷 두 벌(2 suits of clothes) 바지 세 벌(3 pairs of trousers)
도	temperature [2]	영상/영하 삼 도 (3 degrees above/below zero)
곡	song	노래 두 곡(2 songs) 민요 세 곡(3 folk songs)
통	document, letter	편지 한 통(1 letter) 계약서 두 통(2 copies of contract)
곳	place	식당 열 곳(10 restaurants)
뼘	span of hand	세 뼘(3 spans)
움큼	handfull	쌀 다섯 움큼(5 handfull of rice)
점	mark, point [2] ※ in examination	영어 육십 점(60 marks in English) 수학 오 점(5 marks in mathematics)
정	tablet of medicine [1]	소화제 삼/세 정(3 tablets of digestive) 비타민 오/다섯 정(5 tablets of vitamin)
	personal arms [1]	권총 열/십 정(10 revolvers) 기관총 다섯/오 정(5 machine guns)
문	crew-served weapon [1]	박격포 세/삼 문(3 mortars)
발	ammunition [1]	탄약 삼십/서른 발(30 rounds of ammunition)

1 Korean or Chinese 기수 can be used.

2 Only Chinese 기수 can be used.

* The units without sign of 1 or 2 use Korean 기수. But in case of a number bigger than ten, Chinese 기수 can be used.
(트럭 오십이/쉰두/52 대, 사무실 십육/열여섯/16 칸, 소나무 이십오/스물다섯/25 그루, 바지 삼십오/서른다섯/35 벌)

* When Korean 기수 is used as 관형사 →Section13 for counting, the cardinal numbers(하나, 둘, 셋, 넷) change to "한", "두", "세" and "네".
(한 채, 열두 마리, 스물세 그루, 서른네 문)

Note

* The units that are not pure Korean use Chinese 기수. (예: 미터/meter, 킬로미터/kilometer, 파운드/pound, etc.).

* The currency counting(Won/원, peso/페소, dollar/달러, etc.) also uses Chinese 기수.

☐ 나는 필리핀에 집 두 채를 가지고 있다.
I have two houses in the Philippines.

☐ 나는 방학 동안 책 다섯 권을 읽었다.
I read five books during the vacation.

☐ 그는 어젯밤에 맥주 세 병을 마셨다.
He drank three bottles of beer last night.

☐ 말 세 마리가 풀밭에서 풀을 뜯고 있다.
Three horses are grazing in the grass.

☐ 저의 할아버지는 백세까지 사셨습니다.
My grandfather lived until the age of 100, sir.

☐ 우리는 고무장화 네 켤레가 필요하다.
We need four pairs of rubber boots.

☐ 정원에 망고나무 세 그루를 심었습니다.
I planted three mango trees in the garden, sir.

☐ 저는 미국 여행을 여러 번 했습니다.
I have traveled to America several times, sir.

☐ 어제 쌀 세 포대를 샀습니다.
Yesterday I bought three sacks of rice, madam.

- [ ] 돼지고기 다섯 근에 얼마예요?
  How much are five Geuns of pork, aunt?

- [ ] 어제는 세 끼 식사를 라면만 먹었다.
  Yesterday, I ate only ramen for three meals.

- [ ] 나는 어제 편지 두 통을 받았다.
  I reiceved two letters yesterday.

- [ ] 밥 한 공기 더 주세요.
  Please, give me one more bowl of rice.

- [ ] 나는 채소밭에 오이모종 열 포기를 심었다.
  I planted ten seedlings of cucumber in the vegetable garden.

- [ ] 나는 권총으로 열발을/십발을 쏘았다.
  I fired 10 shots with the pistol.

"~씩" and "~당"

1 "씩" adds the meaning of 'each, respectively, apiece' as a suffix(접미사) to the numeral.

- 하나씩: one by one
- 하루에 세 번씩: three times a day
- 나는 매일 여덟 시간씩 일한다.: I work 8 hours every day.
- 이것들은 얼마씩입니까?: How much are these apiece, sir?
- 사과는 한 개에 오백 원씩이다.: The apples are 500Won each.

2 "당" as a suffix adds the meaning of 'per, for each'.

- 인구 일인당(1인당) 국민소득: National income per capita
- 톤당: per ton
- 오징어 한 마리당 삼천 원: 3,000Won per squid
- 입장료는 일인당 이만 원이었다. : The entrance fee was 20,000Won per head.
- 우리는 일인당 삼만 원씩 거두었다(←거두다/collect, gather up).:
  We collected 30,000won per person.

SECTION

12

날짜와 시간

Date and Time

The interrogative expressions about date and time are as follows.

* When?	→ 언제?
* What time?	→ 몇 시?
* How many hours/minutes/seconds?	→ 몇 시간/분/초?
* What date?	→ 며칠?
* How many days?	→ 며칠 동안?
* What day?	→ 무슨 요일?
* What month?	→ 몇 월?
* How many months?	→ 몇 달/개월?
* What season?	→ 무슨 계절?
* What year?	→ 몇 년도?
* How many years?	→ 몇 년?
* How old?	→ 몇 살?
* How long?	→ 얼마나 오래?

1. Expressions of time at the present moment

The question about the time of the moment is;

지금 몇 시야?/지금 몇 시예요?/지금 몇 시입니까?
What time is it now?/-, Mr. ~?/-, sir?

The answers at AM 06:00 for example are;

오전 여섯 시야./오전 여섯 시예요./오전 여섯 시입니다.
It's 6 o'clock in the morning./-, Mr. ~./-, sir.

The unit of time uses the Korean 기수 and the unit of minute and second use the Chinese 기수.

- 01:00 AM → 오전/밤 한 시
- 02:10 AM → 오전/밤 두 시 십 분
- 03:30 AM → 오전/밤 세 시 삼십 분/세 시 반
- 04:40 AM → 오전/새벽 네 시 사십 분
- 05:50 AM → 오전/새벽 다섯 시 오십 분/십 분 전 여섯 시
- 06:00 AM → 오전/아침 여섯 시
- 07:05 AM → 오전/아침 일곱 시 오 분
- 08:15 AM → 오전/아침 여덟 시 십오 분
- 09:25 AM → 오전 아홉 시 이십오 분
- 10:35 AM → 오전 열 시 삼십오 분
- 11:45 AM → 오전/낮 열한 시 사십오 분/십오 분 전 열두 시
- 12:00 AM → 낮 열두 시/정오
- 12:55 AM → 낮 열두 시 오십오 분/오 분 전 한 시
- 01:03 PM → 오후/낮 한 시 삼 분
- 02:13 PM → 오후 두 시 십삼 분
- 05:23 PM → 오후 다섯 시 이십삼 분
- 06:33 PM → 오후/저녁 여섯 시 삼십삼 분
- 07:48 PM → 오후/저녁 일곱 시 사십팔 분/십이 분 전 여덟 시
- 08:58 PM → 오후/밤 여덟 시 오십팔 분/이 분 전 아홉 시
- 11:17 PM → 오후/밤 열한 시 십칠 분
- 12:00 PM → 밤 열두 시/자정
- 12:27 PM → 밤 열두 시 이십칠 분

Words about time of a day

• 밤	night	• 낮	day
• 오전	forenoon, morning	• 오후	afternoon
• 아침	morning	• 저녁	evening
• 새벽	dawn	• 정오	noon
• 자정	midnight	• 주간	daytime
• 야간	nighttime	• 시간	time, hour
• 분	minute	• 초	second
• 한나절	half a day	• 종일/온종일/하루 종일	all day long

☐ 새벽 네 시에 깨워 주세요.
Wake me up at 4 o'clock in the morning, please.

☐ 세 시간 전에 버스는 떠났어.
The bus left three hours ago.

☐ 다섯 시간 후에 만나자.
Let us see in five hours.

☐ 조금 전에 기차는 떠났습니다.
The train left just before, sir.

~(동사)ㄹ 예정이다.
expresses the guess as 단순미래.

☐ 엄마, 잠시 후에 선생님이 도착하실(←도착하시다) 예정이에요.
The teacher will arrive in a while, mommy.

☐ 오후 다섯 시에 우리는 떠난다.
We will leave at five o'clock PM.

☐ 정각 10시에 기차는 출발합니다.
At 10 o'clock sharp the train leaves, sir.

☐ 어제는 종일/온종일/하루 종일 비가 왔다.
It rained yesterday all day long(from morning till night).

2. Expressions regarding the day of week

The interrogative expressions about a day of week are as follows.

☐ 오늘은 무슨 요일이에요?
What day of the week is it today, Mr. ~?

→ 오늘은 일요일이에요.
Today is Sunday, Mr. ~.

☐ 내일은 무슨 요일이야?
What day of the week is it tomorrow?

→ 내일은 수요일이야.
Tomorrow is Wednesday.

☐ 어제는 무슨 요일이었습니까?
What day of the week was it yesterday, sir?

→ 어제는 토요일이었습니다.
Yesterday was Saturday, sir.

Days for a week

Monday	월요일	Tuesday	화요일
Wednesday	수요일	Thursday	목요일
Friday	금요일	Saturday	토요일
Sunday	일요일	one week	일주일
weekday	평일	holiday/regal holiday	공휴일

Words regarding the week

• 금주(이번 주)	this week
• 내주(다음 주)	next week
• 내 내주(다 다음 주)	the week after next
• 전주(지난 주)	last week

• 전전주(지지난 주)	the week before last
• 주말	weekend
• 이번 주말	this weekend
• 다음 주말	next weekend
• 지난 주말	last weekend

- [ ] 일주일은 칠일이다.
  One week is seven days.
- [ ] 우리 가족은 일요일에 성당에 갑니다.
  Our family goes to church on Sunday, sir.
- [ ] 요번 토요일에 뭐 해?
  What are you going to do this Saturday?
- [ ] 지난 일요일에 뭐 했어요?
  What did you do last Sunday, Mrs. ~?
- [ ] 다음 수요일에 뭐 할 거예요?
  What will you do next Wednesday, Mrs. ~?

3. Expressions related to the date

The question about the date of today is "오늘은 며칠이에요?(What is the date today, Mr. ~?).
The order of date in Korean is year(년)-month(월)-day(일).
All the numeral figures of the date are read in Chinese 기수.

Words related to the year

• 연초	beginning of year
• 연말	end of year
• 연말연시	end of year and beginning of year

• 작년	last year
• 재작년	the year before last
• 내년	next year
• 내후년	the year after next
• 올해/금년	this year
• 새해/신년	new year

Months of a year

January	1월(일월)	February	2월(이월)
March	3월(삼월)	April	4월(사월)
May	5월(오월)	June	6월(유월*)
July	7월(칠월)	August	8월(팔월)
September	9월(구월)	October	10월(시월*)
November	11월(십일 월)	December	12월(십이 월)

Words related to the month

• 이번 달/요번 달	this month
• 지난 달	last month
• 다음 달	next month
• 세 달 전/후	three months ago/later
• 월초	beginning of month
• 월말	end of month
• 초순	beginning 10 days of month
• 중순	middle 10 days of month
• 하순	last 10 days of month

Words related to the date

• 오늘	today
• 내일	tomorrow
• 모레	the day after tomorrow
• 글피	two days after tomorrow
• 그글피	three days after tomorrow
• 어제	yesterday
• 그저께	the day before yesterday
• 그끄저께	two days before yesterday

☐ 오늘은 5월 1일이다.
Today is the 1st of May.

☐ 오늘은 무슨 날입니까?
What day is it today, sir?

☐ 오늘은 남편의 생일입니다.
Today is my husband's birthday, madam.

☐ 부인의 생일은 언제입니까?
When is your wife's birthday, sir?

☐ 오늘은 1981년 3월 3일입니다.
Today is the 3. of March 1981, sir.

☐ 저는 2002년 11월 27일에 태어났습니다.
I was born on November 27th 2002, sir.

☐ 저는 다음 달에 한국으로 여행가요.
I'm traveling to Korea next month, Mr. ~.

☐ 한 달은 30일 또는 31일이다.
One month is thirty or thirty-one days.

- When counting days such as one day, two days, three days, etc, Chinese cardinal or pure Korean counting words for days are used together.

  - Chinese cardinal

    1(일)일, 2(이)일, 3(삼)일……

  - Pure Korean counting words for days

    하루(1), 이틀(2), 사흘(3), 나흘(4), 닷새(5), 엿새(6), 이레(7), 여드레(8), 아흐레(9), 열흘(10), 열하루(11), 열이틀(12), 열사흘(13), 열나흘(14), 열닷새(15)…

    ※ Counting with Chinese cardinal is used more often.

    ※ Nowadays, pure Korean counting words are usually used less than "이레(7 days)".

4. Four seasons (사계절)

- 봄 spring(3월~5월)
- 여름 summer(6월~8월)
- 가을 autumn(9월~11월)
- 겨울 winter(12월~2월)

☐ 봄은 꽃이 피는 계절이다.
Spring is a flowering season.

☐ 한국은 사계절이 완전히 다르다.
The four seasons in Korea are completely different.

☐ 한국의 여름은 필리핀처럼 덥다.
The summer of Korea is as hot as the Philippines.

☐ 가을은 독서의 계절이다.
Autumn is a season for reading.

☐ 겨울은 눈이 오는 계절이다.
Winter is a season for snowing.

□ 눈이 오는 자연의 경치는 정말 아름답다.
The natural scenery of snowing is really beautiful.

5. "~ 전에(before, ago)" and "~ 후에/다음에(after, later)"

1 (명사)~ 전에 (동명사)~기 전에 (명사형 서술격조사)~(이)기 전에

- 동명사: Gerund → Section 14
- 명사형 서술격조사: Noun form of 서술격조사

□ 식사하기(←식사하다) 전에 손을 씻어라./식사 전에 손을 씻어라.
Wash your hands before you eat.

□ 한 시간 전에 이미 기차는 떠났다.
One hour ago, the train left already.

□ 삼 년 전에 할아버지는 세상을 떠나셨다.
Three years ago, grandpa passed away.

□ 그 사람도 선생님이기(←선생님이다) 전에 인간이다.
That person is also a human being before as being a teacher.

□ 잠자기(←잠자다) 전에 항상 양치질을 합니다.
I brush always my teeth before I go to bed, sir.

□ 죽기(←죽다) 전에 유언장을 변호사에게 맡기겠다.
I will leave my will to a lawyer before I die.

2 (명사)~ 후에
(동사적 관형사 of 과거시제)~ㄴ 후에/다음에

• 동사적 관형사: Verbal pre-noun → Section 13

☐ 나는 식사한(←식사하다) 후에/다음에 티브이를 본다.

나는 식사 후에 티브이를 본다.
I watch TV after eating.

☐ 한 시간 후에 기차는 출발할 것이다.
One hour later, the train will leave.

☐ 삼 년 정도 후에 한국은 통일될 것이다.
After about three years, Korea will be unified.

☐ 할아버지가 돌아가신(←돌아가시다) 후에/다음에 할머니는 매일 우신다(←울다).
The grandmother weeps every day after grandfather passed away.

☐ 내가 질문한(←질문하다) 후에/다음에 말해라.
Say after I ask.

☐ 방과 후에 뭐 해?
What do you do after school?

SECTION

13 관형사

Pre-noun

관형사 modifies the following 체언 with the characteristics of no inflection and no 조사 and is classified as follows.

- 수관형사: Numeral pre-noun
- 지시관형사: Demonstrative pre-noun
- 소유격 관형사: Genitive pre-noun
- 성상관형사: Specifying pre-noun
  - 순수관형사: Pure pre-noun
  - 동사적 관형사: Verbal pre-noun
  - 형용사적 관형사: Adjectival pre-noun

Note

1. The adjective in 영어 corresponds to two 품사 in 한국어, which are 관형사 and 형용사.
2. 형용사 corresponds to the predicative adjective and 형용사적 관형사 corresponds to the limiting adjective in 영어.

1. 수관형사

1 All numerals for counting before units in Section 11

• 다섯 시간	five hours	• 승용차 세 대	three cars
• 꽃 열 송이	ten flowers	• 수박 일곱 통	seven watermelon
• 옥수수 오 키로	five kilos of corn		

2 Etcetera

• 여러 의견	several opinions
• 모든 사람들	all of the people
• 갖가지 야채	several kinds of vegetable
• 몇 사람	some persons
• 많은 학생들	many students
• 적은 수입	small income
• 한두(두세, 서너, 너덧, 대여섯, 예닐곱) 개	one or two(two o three, three or four, five or six, six or seven) pieces

2. 지시관형사

1 이(this), 그(that), 저(that) and 아무(any)

→ Section 6

2 The derivatives of above

• 이러한/이런 사람	person like this
• 그러한/그런 의견	opinion like that
• 저러한/저런 행동	behavior like that
• 아무런 ~ 없다.	really none, without any

- [ ] 아무런 차이가 없다.
  There is really no difference.

- [ ] 이것은 아무런 가치가 없다.
  This is thoroughly worthless.

3 관형사 for interrogation

Refer to "무슨(what), 어떤(what kind of), 어느(which), 몇(how many), 몇째(what number of)" of 의문사 의문문. → Section 9

3. 소유격관형사: 체언 + "의"

• 나의(내) 남동생/여동생	my younger brother/sister
• 너의(네) 형/오빠	your elder brother
• 아버지의 모자	father's hat
• 학교의 정문	main gate of school
• 한국의 대통령	president of Korea
• 비행기의 속도	speed of airplane

* Mostly in the colloquial expression, "의" of 소유격관형사 is omitted such as "아버지 모자", "학교 정문", "한국 대통령" and "비행기 속도".

* "형" and "형님(honorific title of "형")" mean the elder brother to younger brother, and "오빠" means the elder brother to younger sister.

* "누나" and "누님(honorific title of "누나")" as antonyms to "형" and "형님" mean elder sister to younger brother. "언니" as an antonym to "오빠" means the elder sister to younger sister.

4. 성상관형사

성상관형사 specifies the nature or state of the object.

1 순수관형사

• 새/헌 공책	new/old notebook
• 왼/오른 손	left/right hand
• 지난/다음 달	last/next month
• 옛 집/친구/추억	old house/friend/memories
• 이번 달/방학/선거	this month/vacation/election
• 외딴 곳/섬/집	secluded place/solitary island/isolated house
• 맨 꼭대기	the highest place
• 맨 먼저	very first of all
• 맨 앞자리/뒷자리	the very front seat/the very rear seat

• And so on.

2 동사적 관형사

example (부정사)	미래시제 (~ㄹ/~을)	현재시제 (~는)	과거시제 (~ㄴ/~은)	대과거시제 (~았던/~었던)
가다 (go)	갈	가는	간	갔던
오다 (come)	올	오는	온	왔던
먹다, 드시다 (eat)	먹을, 드실	먹는, 드시는	먹은, 드신	먹었던, 드셨던
쓰다 (write, use)	쓸	쓰는	쓴	썼던
보다 (see, watch)	볼	보는	본	보았던
삼키다 (swallow)	삼킬	삼키는	삼킨	삼켰던
따르다 (follow)	따를	따르는	따른	따랐던

말하다 (say, tell, speak)	말할	말하는	말한	말했던
포함하다 (include)	포함할	포함하는	포함한	포함했던
표현하다 (express)	표현할	표현하는	표현한	표현했던
싸우다 (fight, quarrel)	싸울	싸우는	싸운	싸웠던
빠지다 (fall into, drown)	빠질	빠지는	빠진	빠졌던

- [ ] 지금은 학교에 갈 시간이다.
  Now is the time to go to school.

- [ ] 어제 온 사람은 나의 친척이다.
  The person who came yesterday is my relative.

- [ ] 빵을 드실 분은 지금 말하세요.
  Tell me now if anyone wants to eat bread, please.

- [ ] 너에게 편지를 쓴 사람은 나다.
  I am the person who wrote you the letter.

- [ ] 이 영화는 내가 지금까지 보았던 영화 중에 최고로 재미있다.
  This movie is the most interesting of all the movies that I've watched so far.

- [ ] 나는 동전을 삼켰던 경험이 있다.
  I have an experience that I swallowed a coin.

- [ ] 그렇게 말한 학생은 영철이다.
  Yeongcheol is the student who spoke that way.

- [ ] 나는 그를 우리의 모임에 포함할 것이다.
  I will include him in our meeting.

- [ ] 심장을 의미하는 몸짓은 사랑을 표현하는 방법이다.
  The gesture that means the heart is a way of expressing love.

- [ ] 우리는 적과 싸울 준비가 필요하다.
  We need to prepare to fight the enemy.

3 형용사적 관형사

Examples of 형용사	현재시제 (~ㄴ)	과거시제 (~았던, ~었던)	대과거시제 (~ㅆ었던)
아름답다, 예쁘다 (beautiful)	아름다운, 예쁜	아름다웠던, 예뻤던	아름다웠었던, 예뻤었던
뚱뚱하다 (fat)	뚱뚱한	뚱뚱했던	뚱뚱했었던
날씬하다 (slim)	날씬한	날씬했던	날씬했었던
크다 (big)	큰	컸던	컸었던
작다 (small)	작은	작았던	작았었던
둥글다 (round)	둥근	둥글었던	둥글었었던
날카롭다 (sharp)	날카로운	날카로웠던	날카로웠었던
밝다 (bright)	밝은	밝았던	밝았었던
어둡다 (dark)	어두운	어두웠던	어두웠었던

- 미래시제 is possible in the form of "(형용사)~ㄹ" (아름다울, 뚱뚱할, 클, 어두울, etc.), but is mostly used when modifying the incomplete noun(의존명사: 것, 수, etc. →Section 14).

"때" means "when" as 명사.

☐ 그는 아름다운 아내가 있다.
He has a beautiful wife.

☐ 초등학생이었을(←초등학생이었다.) 때, 그녀는 예뻤었던 소녀였다.
When she was in elementary school, she had been a pretty girl.

☐ 뚱뚱한 남자가 빵을 먹고 있었어요.
A fat man was eating bread, Mr. ~.

"~면" of "되면(←되다: become)" and "~서" of "자라서(←자라다: grow up)" are the connective 어미.
→Section 21, 22

☐ 그 소녀는 처녀가 되면 매우 예쁠 것이다.
The girl will be very pretty when she becomes a maiden.

☐ 그 소녀는 자라서, 예쁜 처녀가 될(← 되다, become) 것이다.
The girl will grow up and become a pretty maiden.

☐ 나는 날씬한 여자가 좋다.
I like a slim woman.

☐ 그는 큰 집에서 삽니다.
He lives in a big house, sir.

☐ 둥글었던 달이 반달이 되었다.
The round moon became half moon.

반짝이다: shine, glitter

☐ 어두운 길에서 반짝이는(←반짝이다) 동전을 주웠다(←줍다).
I picked up a shiny coin on the dark road.

Note

The order of 관형사

1) 지시관형사 + 성상관형사
 - 이 새 옷 : this new clothes

2) 지시관형사 + 수관형사
 - 저 네 아들 : those four sons

3) 수관형사 + 성상관형사
 - 두 예쁜 딸 : two beautiful daughters

4) 지시관형사 + 수관형사 + 성상관형사
 - 그 두 헌 창고 : those two old storehouses

SECTION

14

명사

Noun

명사 can be classified into many categories. Among them, two complicate types which are Incomplete noun(의존명사) and Derived noun(파생명사) will be explained here .

1. 의존명사

의존명사 which is a unique point in 한국어 is the antonym of Independent noun(자립명사) which means all ordinary 명사. 의존명사 cannot be used alone, so always together with 관형사 or 명사 as a preceding word.

(1) All units for counting in Section 11 are 의존명사 because a numeral is needed as 관형사.
(2) "~ 씨", "~ 님", "~ 군" and "~ 양' when calling name politely with honorific formality in the vocative case(→Section 4) are 의존명사 since personal name is required as a preceding word.
(3) Others of 의존명사

것	thing, fact, action

- ☐ 작은 것이 필요하다.
  Small things are needed.
- ☐ 어느 것이 좋으냐?
  Which one do you prefer?
- ☐ 아침 일찍 일어나는 것은 쉽지 않다.
  Getting up early in the morning is not easy.

격	instance, like, as it were

- ☐ 다 된 밥에 재 뿌리는 격이다.
  It's like sprinkling ashes on cooked rice.
- ☐ 소 잃고 외양간 고치는 격이다.
  That is an instance of fixing the stable after the cow is stolen.
- ☐ 그것은 공중에 누각을 짓는(← 짓다/build) 격이다.
  That is, as it were, building a castle in the air.

"격" is often used when speaking in analogy to proverb.

겸	concurrence, addition, simultaneity

- ☐ 친구도 만나고 산책도 할 겸 공원에 갔다.
  I went to the park to meet with a friend, in addition to take a walk.

☐ 영어공부도 할 겸 미국 FOX방송의 뉴스를 보고 있다.
I am watching the news from FOX channel of US, and to learn English as well.

☐ 친구도 사귈(←사귀다) 겸 등산동호회에 참가했다.
I joined an association of mountain climbing, in addition to make friends.

☐ 총리 겸 외무부 장관
Prime Minister and concurrently Minister of Foreign Affairs

The preceding word is 명사 or 관형사(~ㄹ).

☐ 침실 겸 서재
bedroom and concurrently studyroom

곳/데	place

☐ 어느 곳이 좋을까?
Which place is good?

☐ 앉을 데를/곳을 찾아라.
Find a place to sit.

☐ 내가 자는 곳은/데는 여기다.
This is where I sleep.

김	chance, opportunity

☐ 생각난 김에 너에게 전화했다.
I called you on the chance I thought of you.

☐ 나온 김에 쇼핑하자.
Let us go shopping while we are out.

☐ 청소하는 김에 내 방도 치워주겠어(←치워주다)?
Could you tidy up my room, while you are cleaning yours?

나름 1	dependence

☐ 아내의 친절은 남편이 하기 나름이다.
A wife's kindness is up to her husband's attitude.

☐ 월급은 네가 열심히 일하기 나름이다.
The salary depends on how hard you work.

The preceding word is 명사.

☐ 그것은 사람 나름이다.
That depends on the person.

나름 2	one's own way

☐ 그는 항상 자기 나름대로 한다.
He always does in his own way.

☐ 그는 그 사람 나름의 수영법으로 우승했다.
He won the championship by his own swimming method.

The preceding word is 명사.

대로	in accordance, following

☐ 아이들은 어른들이 행동하는 대로 따라(←따르다) 한다.
Children act as adults do.

☐ 내가 시킨(← 시키다) 대로 해라.
Do as I have told you.

☐ 학생들은 선생님이 말하는 대로 노트에 쓴다.
The students write in the notebook as the teacher says.

"~대로 → Section 15 부사격조사

"시키다" is a causative verb. → Section 20

동안	period of time, while, during

☐ 자고 있는 동안(에) 버스는 서울에 도착했다.
The bus arrived in Seoul while sleeping.

☐ 걷는 동안(에) 많은 생각을 했습니다.
I thought a lot while walking, sir.

☐ 여름방학 동안(에) 미국을 여행하였다.
I traveled to the US during summer vacation.

The preceding word is 명사 or 관형사(~ㄴ).

부사격조사 of "~에" from "동안에" for specifying a period of time can be omitted.

듯	likeliness, as if

☐ 그 사람도 함께 갈 듯이 말했다.
The person said as if he will go also together.

☐ 그는 올 듯 말(안 올) 듯 말했어요.
He said as if he would come or not come, Mr. ~.

☐ 내일 비가 올 듯 말(안 올) 듯하다.
There's no telling whether it will rain or not tomorrow.

☐ 밥이 적어 먹은 듯 만(안 먹은) 듯하다.
There was so little rice that I hardly feel as if I had eaten any.

*The preceding word is 명사.

때문 reason, cause

- [ ] 너 때문에 학교에 늦었다.
  Because of you, I was late for school.

- [ ] 바쁘기 때문에 시간이 없어요.
  Because I'm busy, I don't have time.

- [ ] 교통사고 때문에 학교에 지각했다.
  Due to a traffic accident, I was late for school.

리 reason for negation or counter–question

- [ ] 그는 부자이기 때문에 돈을 빌릴(←빌리다) 리가 없다.
  Because he is rich, there is no reason to borrow money.

- [ ] 그는 착하기 때문에 나쁜 행동을 할 리가 없다.
  Because he is good, there is no reason to act badly.

- [ ] 그게(←그것이) 정말일(←정말이다) 리가 없다.
  That can't be true.

- [ ] 그럴(←그렇다) 리가 있나?
  How can that be?

마련 natural affair, inevitability

- [ ] 사람은 죽기/죽게(←죽다/die) 마련이다.
  For human the death is a natural affair.

- [ ] 겨울은 춥기 마련이다.
  It is natural that the winter is cold.

동사 is derived to "~기" or "~게" to be a preceding word.

- [ ] 돈이 있으면 쓰기/쓰게(←쓰다/spend, consume, use) 마련이다.
  If there is money, spending is a natural thing.

만큼 as ~ as, equal to, so much

- [ ] 주는 만큼 받는다.
  You receive as much as you give.

- [ ] 열심히 일하는 만큼 월급을 받는다.
  As much as you work hard, you get paid.

"만큼" → Section 15
부사격조사

☐ 이 만큼 주세요.
Give me this much, Mr. ~!

모양	sign, symptom

* As 자립명사, "모양" means 'shape, appearance, etc.'.

☐ 오늘은 비가 올 모양이다.
It looks like rain today.

☐ 그는 곧 떠날 모양이다.
He seems to leave soon.

바	thing(→것), content, concern

☐ 내가 아는 바를/것을 말하겠다.
I'll tell you what I know.

☐ 당신이 생각하는 바는/것은 무엇입니까.
What is the content of your mind, sir?

☐ 그는 할 바를 모른다.
He does not know what to do.

☐ 그것은 네가 알 바 아니다.
It is no concern of yours./It's none of your business.

바람	motive, consequence, result

As 자립명사, "바람" means wind or desire.

☐ 너무 서두르는 바람에 열쇠를 잊었다.
Because I was in a hurry, I forgot the key.

☐ 급히 먹는 바람에 체했다.
Because of eating fast, I have an upset stomach.

☐ 아이들이 떠드는(← 떠들다) 바람에 잠이 깼다.
As a result of confusion by children, I woke up.

뿐/따름	only, just

* "그냥, 단지": 부사 → Section 18

☐ 나는 그것을 그냥 들었을 뿐이다./따름이다.
I just heard that.

* "만, 뿐": 보조사 → Section 15

☐ 단지 하나만 있을 따름이다./뿐이다.
There is only one.

수	capability, possibility

□ 나는 학교에 갈 수 없다.
I can't go to school.

□ 그는 영자 신문을 읽을 수 있다.
He can read an English newspaper.

□ 그것은 있을 수 없는 일이다.
It is out of the bounds of possibility./It's impossible.

적	the time when ~, experience in the past

□ 그가 왔을 적에 난 없었다.
When he came, I was away.

□ 나는 필리핀에 간 적이 없다.
I have never been to the Philippines.

□ 나는 이 음식을 한 번 먹은 적이 있다.
I have eaten this food once.

줄	capability, knowledge

□ 영어 할 줄 알아?/영어 할 수 있어?
Can you speak English?

□ 그는 수영을 할 줄 안다./그는 수영을 할 수 있다.
He knows how to swim./He can swim.

□ 그가 집에 있는 줄 알았다./몰랐다.
I thought that he was at home./I didn't know he was at home.

□ 그는 글을 쓸 줄 모른다.
He does not know how to write.

중 → Section 7	while, progressive, amid

The preceding word is 명사 or 관형사(~ㄴ).

□ 지금 식사하는 중이다./식사 중이다.
I am at table now.

□ 아버님은 지금 산책하는 중이십니다./산책 중이십니다.
Father is taking a walk now, sir.

□ 할아버지는 지금 주무시는 중이시다.
Grandpa is sleeping now.

□ 그것은 불행 중 다행이다.
It's a bright spot in the misfortune.

지	since, from the time

□ 도착한 지 세 시간 되었습니다.
It's been three hours since I arrived, sir.

□ 이 회사에 입사한 지 십 년이 지났다.
Ten years have passed since I joined this company.

□ 햇빛을 본 지 오래되었다.
It's been a long time since I saw sunlight.

"막" means 'just, right at the time' as 부사.
→ Section 18

참	just before the moment

□ 지금 막 식사를 시작하려는(←시작하려고 하는) 참이다.
I'm just about to start eating.

□ 잠이 막 들려는(←들려고 하는) 참이었다.
I was on the verge of falling asleep.

채	as it is, without changing

□ 나는 전등을 켠(←켜다) 채로 잤다.
I slept with the light on.

□ 그는 앉은 채로 손님에게 인사했다.
In sitting position, he greeted the visitor(without standing up).

□ 그는 선 채로 밥을 먹고 있다.
In standing position, he is eating the meal(without sitting down).

체/척	pretense, act of pretending

□ 그는 나를 못 본 체한다./척한다.
He pretends not to see me.

□ 잘난 체하지/척하지 마라.
Don't pretend you're somebody

□ 잠자는 체하자./척하자.
Let's pretend to be asleep.

통 situation by something happened

The preceding word is 명사 or 관형사(~ㄴ).

□ 전화가 오는 통에 잠이 깼다.
I woke up to a phone call.

□ 바람이 부는 통에 모자가 날아갔다.
The hat was blown away by the wind.

□ 전쟁 통에 많은 사람이 죽었다.
Many lives are lost in the of war.

판 negative circumstance by something happened

□ 빚 때문에 차를 팔아야 할 판이다.
Due to the debt I'm in the circumstance of selling my car.

□ 결혼비용 때문에 은행에서 돈을 빌려야 할 판이다.
Because of wedding expenses, I'm in the situation of borrowing money from the bank.

□ 너무 추워서 얼어 죽을 판이다.
It was so cold that I almost froze to death.

편 rather, tending to, side, facilities

The preceding word is 명사 or 관형사(~ㄴ).

□ 저는 뚱뚱한 편이다.
I'm rather fat.

□ 나는 매운 음식을 잘 먹는 편이다.
I tend to eat spicy foods well.

"좀" is 준말 of "조금/slightly, a little, a bit)".

□ 그분은 좀 엄한(←엄하다/strict, stern) 편이다.
He is a little on the strict side.

□ 철수는 기차 편으로 부산에 갔다.
Cheolsu went to Busan by train.

2. 파생명사

1 Examples of 파생명사 from 용언

- 삶(life), 사람(human-being), 살림(livelihood/household) ← 살다(live)
- 그림(drawing) ← 그리다(draw a picture: 그림을 그리다)
- 춤(dancing) ← 추다(dance: 춤추다, 춤을 추다)
- 꿈(dream) ← 꾸다(dream: 꿈꾸다, 꿈을 꾸다)
- 얼음(ice) ← 얼다(freeze, ice)
- 노름(gambling) ← 놀다(play)
- 잠(sleep) ← 자다(sleep, go to sleep: 잠자다, 잠을 자다)
- 이름(name) ← 이르다(call)
- 짐(burden), 지게(jige) ← 지다(carry on the back)
- 걸음(step) ← 걷다(walk, go on foot)
- 울음(crying) ← 울다(cry)
- 웃음(laugh/laughter) ← 웃다(laugh)
- 싸움(fighting) ← 싸우다(fight)
- 숨(breath) ← 쉬다(draw a breath: 숨을 쉬다)
- 부채(fan) ← 부치다(use a fan: 부채로 부치다)
- 덮개(cover) ← 덮다(cover)
- 마개(stopper) ← 막다(stop up)
- 지우개(eraser) ← 지우다(erase)
- 집게(tongs) ← 집다(pick up)
- 추위(coldness) ← 춥다(cold)
- 더위(heat) ← 덥다(hot)

지게(jige)
Korean traditional tool for transportation which is carried on the back of person.

2 Gerund(동명사): (어간 of 동사)~기, ~ㅁ, ~는 것

- 가다(go) → 가기, 감, 가는 것
- 그리다(draw a picture) → 그리기, 그리는 것
- 추다(dance) → 추기, 추는 것
- 걷다(walk) → 걷기, 걷는 것
- 공부하다(study) → 공부하기, 공부함, 공부하는 것
- 쓰다(write) → 쓰기, 씀, 쓰는 것
- 지키다(watch) → 지키기, 지킴, 지키는 것
- 샤워하다(take a shower) → 샤워하기, 샤워함, 샤워하는 것
- 더하다(add) → 더하기, 더함, 더하는 것
- 빼다(subtract) → 빼기, 뺌, 빼는 것

• 곱하다(multiply) → 곱함, 곱하는 것
• 나누다(divide) → 나누기, 나눔, 나누는 것
• And so on from all of 동사.

3 Adjectival noun(형용명사): (어간 of 형용사)~기, ~ㅁ

• 푸르다(blue) → 푸르기/푸름(blueness)
• 아름답다(beautiful) → 아름답기/아름다움(beauty)
• 빠르다(fast) → 빠르기/빠름(fastness)
• 젊다(young) → 젊기/젊음(youth)
• 밝다(bright) → 밝기/밝음(brightness)
• 슬프다(sad) → 슬프기/슬픔(sadness)
• 자유롭다(free) → 자유롭기/자유로움(being free, freedom)
• 정직하다(honest) → 정직하기/정직함(honesty, being honest)
• 깨끗하다(clean) → 깨끗하기/깨끗함(cleanliness)
• And so on from all of 형용사

형용명사 should be understood and used as the same way as 동명사.

4 Examples of 파생명사 by affix(접사) to 어근(word-root)

1 맏~: firstborn, first, eldest

• 맏딸: the eldest daughter
• 맏형: the eldest brother
• 맏사위: the first son-in-law
• 맏아들: the eldest son
• 맏며느리: the first daughter-in-law

2 홀~: single, unmarried, odd

• 홀몸: single person, unmarried person
• 홀아버지(홀아비): widower
• 홀시어머니: single mother-in-law
• 홀어머니(홀어미): widow
• 홀시아버지: single father-in-law
• 홀수: odd number
(↔짝수: even number)

3 풋~: green, unripe, inexperienced, immature

• 풋고추: unripe(green) pepper
• 풋과일: unripe fruits
• 풋사과: unripe(green) apple
• 풋사랑: puppy(calf) love
• 풋내기: inexperienced person, greenhorn, beginner

4 맨~: bare, naked

- 맨눈: eyes without glasses
- 맨몸: body only (nothing together)
- 맨발: bare feet
- 맨손: bare(empty) hand
- 맨입: empty mouth, speech only without any other realty
- 맨바닥: bare floor
- 맨주먹: naked fist

4 암/암ㅎ~: female

- 암놈/암컷: female creature
- 암탉: hen
- 암소: cow
- 암캐: female dog
- 암고양이: female cat
- 암퇘지: female hog
- 암수: female and male
- 암나사: nut, female screw

6 수/수ㅎ~: male

- 수놈/수컷: male creature
- 수캐: male dog
- 수탉: cock
- 수소: ox
- 수고양이: male cat
- 수퇘지: male hog
- 수나사: bolt, male screw

7 노~: old, aged

- 노인: an old(aged) person
- 노총각: old bachelor
- 노처녀: old virgin
- 노신사: old gentleman

8 ~꾸러기/쟁이: person who overdoes something habitually or overindulges oneself

The suffix of "~꾸러기" is usually used for children.

- 잠꾸러기: sleepyhead, heavy sleeper
- 장난꾸러기: naughty child
- 심술꾸러기/심술쟁이: crosspatch, ill-natured person
- 욕심꾸러기/욕심쟁이: selfish/greedy person, hog
- 변덕꾸러기/변덕쟁이: capricious person, man of moods
- 겁쟁이: coward, mouse
- 거짓말쟁이: liar
- 수다쟁이: talkative person, chatterbox
- 멋쟁이: dandy, fop, dude, classy dresser

9 ~보: person who overdoes something habitually or has a physical defect

- 울보: crybaby, blubberer
- 느림보: laggard, slow coach
- 땅딸보: dumpy/stocky person
- 털보: hairy/shaggy person
- 먹보: greedyguts
- 꾀보: tricky/wily person
- 뚱뚱보: fat person
- 째보: harelipped person
- 곰보: pockmarked person

10 ~가/사: professional person

- 전문가: specialist
- 작가: writer, author
- 화가: painter, artist
- 의사: doctor, medical man
- 변호사: lawyer
- 박사: doctor, Ph. D.
- 항해사: navigation officer
- 사업가: businessman
- 극작가: scriptwriter, playwright
- 소설가: novelist
- 교사: teacher
- 간호사: nurse
- 판사: judge
- 비행사: aviator

11 ~꾼: person who has a secular job or does something habitually

- 장사꾼: trader, merchant
- 구경꾼: spectator, audience
- 일꾼: laborer, worker
- 나무꾼: woodman, firewood gatherer
- 싸움꾼: man of combative spirit, fire-eating man
- 노름꾼: gambler
- 사기꾼: swindler, defrauder
- 짐꾼: carrier, porter
- 낚시꾼: angler

12 ~질: act of doing

- 양치질: brushing the teeth
- 가위질: scissoring
- 톱질: sawing
- 도둑질: stealing, theft
- 서방질: adultery
- 바느질: needlework, sewing
- 도끼질: wielding an ax
- 손가락질: pointing one's finger
- 계집질: womanizing, whoring

13 숫~: innocent, unspoiled

- 숫총각: innocent bachelor
- 숫처녀: immaculate virgin

3. Examples of monosyllabic noun (단음절명사)

* The word in parenthesis( ) is the word of foreign origin.

1 Body related

- 귀: ear
- 넋: soul, spirit
- 눈: eye
- 등: back
- 목: neck
- 몸: body
- 발: foot
- 배: belly, abdomen, stomach
- 볼/뺨: cheek
- 뼈: bone
- 뿔: horn
- 살: flesh
- 손: hand
- 위(胃): stomach
- 입: mouth
- 코: nose
- 키: stature, height
- 턱: jaw
- 털: hair
- 팔: arm
- 폐(肺): lung
- 피: blood
- 혀: tongue
- 혹: lump, swelling, wen
- 혼(魂): soul, spirit

2 Creatures with heart

- 개: dog
- 곰: bear
- 나: I
- 남: another person, stranger
- 너: you
- 닭: chicken
- 딸: daughter
- 말: horse
- 뱀: snake
- 벌: bee
- 벗: friend
- 새: bird
- 소: cattle(bull, cow)
- 신(神): God
- 양(羊): sheep
- 용(龍): dragon
- 학(鶴): crane

3 Creatures without heart

- 강(江): river
- 금(金): gold
- 김: laver, seaweed
- 달: moon
- 돌: stone
- 들: plain, uncultivated field
- 땅: earth, ground, land
- 무: radish
- 물: water
- 벼: rice plant
- 별: star
- 산(山): mountain
- 섬: island
- 은(銀): silver
- 차(茶): tea
- 파: leek, green onion
- 풀: grass, plant
- 해: sun
- 흙: earth, soil

4 Proucts from creatures

- 감: persimmon
- 귤: orange
- 김: steam, vapor
- 꽃: flower
- 꿀: honey
- 낮: daytime
- 눈: snow
- 땀: sweat
- 떡: rice-cake
- 똥: excrement, dung
- 밤: chestnut
- 밤: nighttime
- 병(病): disease, sickness
- 봄: spring
- 비: rain
- 빛: light
- 솜: cotton
- 쇠: iron, metal
- 쌀: rice
- 암(癌): cancer
- 잎: leaf
- 잣: pine nuts
- 침: saliva
- 콩: bean

SECTION

15

PP: 조사

Postposition

In this section we will learn one of the two most complicate parts which are 조사 for 체언 and 어미변화(inflection of word-ending) for 용언. These are the main differences of 한국어 that is an agglutinative language(교착어) from 영어 that is an inflectional language(굴절어). 조사 is written without space behind 체언 and functions as a conjunctive to the following word.

The types of 조사 are as follows.

- 격조사: PP for case
  - 주격조사: Subjective PP
  - 목적격조사: Objective PP
  - 보격조사: Complementary PP
  - 관형격조사: Pre-nominal PP
  - 부사격조사: Adverbial PP
  - 서술격조사: Predicative PP
  - 호격조사: Vocative PP
- 보조사: Auxiliary PP

1. 격조사

격조사 is used to express the case of 체언 without extra meaning. In the colloquial style, 격조사 for 주격, 목적격, 보격 and 관형격 can be omitted because the case of 체언 is already recognized from the position of 체언 in the sentence.

1 주격조사

1 **주격조사** are "~이" and "~가"(→Section 4) which are used to express that the **체언** is subjective case. "~은" and "~는" are classified as **보조사** that can be used instead of "~이" and "~가" to add some extra meaning to the sentence.

2 **~께서**: Used to be respectful to the 3. person.

"~에" is a 부사격조사 which is used for place, time, direction, etc.

- [ ] 할아버지께서 그렇게 말씀하셨어.
  The grandfather said so.
- [ ] 오늘 회의에 사장님께서 참석하실 예정입니다.
  The boss is expected to attend today's meeting, sir.
- [ ] 할머니께서 지금 주무시고 계십니다.
  Grandmother is sleeping now, sir.

3 **~에서**: Used very often as **부사격조사** which means "at/in/from a place", but when the subject is a name of organization such as school, company, government and so on, it can be used as **주격조사**.

"~고 합니다.(←~고 하다)" expresses the indirect speech(간접화법).

- [ ] 회사에서 월급을 올린다고 합니다.
  It is said that the company will raise salaries, sir.
- [ ] 이것은 정부에서 추진하는 사업이다.
  This is a project which the government is promoting.
- [ ] 내일 학교에서 소풍을 갑니다.
  Tomorrow the students of the school will go picnic, sir.

4 Omission of 주격조사 in colloquial style

- 영수는 뭐해요? → 영수 뭐해요?
  What is Yeongsu doing, Mr. ~?
- 아버님은 집에 안 계십니다. → 아버님 집에 안 계십니다.
  Father is not home, sir.
- 사장님은 언제 돌아오세요? → 사장님 언제 돌아오세요?
  When does the president come back, Miss ~?

5 Abbreviation of "~는"

"~는" is often abbreviated in colloquial style when combined to the pronouns(나/저/너/우리/저희/너희, 이것/그것/저것, 여기/거기/저기 →Section 6).

* 너는 → 넌, 우리는 → 우린, 저희는 → 저흰, 너희는 → 너흰
* 그것은 → 그건, 저것은 → 저건
* 거기는 → 거긴, 저기는 → 저긴

- 난(← 나는) 영호를 좋아한다.
  I like Yeongho.
- 이건(← 이것은) 순희의 공책이다.
  This is Sunhi's notebook.
- 여긴(← 여기는) 왜 왔어?
  Why did you come here?

2 목적격조사 →Section 4(Formula 4)

1 Omission of 목적격조사 in colloquial style

- 철수가 영미를 좋아한다. → 철수 영미 좋아한다.
  Cheolsu likes Yeongmi.
- 지금 맥주를 마시고 있다. → 지금 맥주 마시고 있다.
  I am drinking beer now.
- 오늘 영화를 보러 갈 예정이다. → 오늘 영화 보러 갈 예정이다.
  I am going to see a movie today.

2 Abbreviation of "~를"

In colloquial style, when "~를" is combined with pronouns(나/저/너/우리/저희/너희/누구, 이것/저것/그것), "~를" is often abbreviated.

- 난 널(← 너를) 사랑해.
  I love you.

- 넌 누굴(← 누구를) 좋아하느냐?
  Who do you like?

나를 → 날, 저를 → 절, 저희를 → 저흴, 너희를 → 너흴 그것을→그걸, 저것을→저걸

- 선생님이 우릴(← 우리를) 기다리신다.
  The teacher is waiting for us.

- 나는 이걸(←이것을) 너에게 주겠다.
  I will give you this.

3 보격조사 →Section 4(Formula 2)

1 Omission of 보격조사 in colloquial style

•너는 어른이 된다. → 너는/넌 어른 된다.
•구름이 비가 된다. → 구름이 비 된다.
•이것은 옷이 아니다. → 이것은/이건 옷 아니다.

4 관형격조사

→Section 13[Genitive pre-noun(소유격 관형사)]

5 부사격조사

부사격조사 corresponds to the preposition(at, between, by. in, of, on, to...) of 영어 and converts 체언 to 부사어 which modifies the following 서술어.

~에	place where exists

- 나의 가족은 한국에 살고 있다.
  My family lives in Korea.

☐ 할머니는 거실에 계세요. 아빠.
Granny is in the living room, daddy.

☐ 형은 지금 집에 없다.
My elder brother is not at home now.

~에서	place where acts

☐ 할아버지는 방에서 주무시고 계십니다.
Grandpa is sleeping in the room, sir.

☐ 운동장에서 축구를 했다.
I played soccer with friends in the playground.

☐ 저는 어디에서 자요?
Where do I sleep, aunt?

~에	place to act on

☐ 피곤하면 침대에 누워라(← 눕다).
If tired, lie on the bed!

☐ 엄마는 쟁반을 탁자에 놓았다.
Mom put a tray on the table.

~에서, ~에서부터	receding from place or thing

"~에서부터" expresses the exact place where to depart.

☐ 미국에서 친척이 왔어요.
Relatives came from the states, Mr. ~.

☐ 어디에서 오셨습니까?
Where are you from, sir?

☐ 나는 기차역에서부터 걸었다.
I walked from the train station.

~에, ~(으)로	approaching to place or thing

☐ 드디어 집에 도착했다.
At last, I arrived home.

"~(으)로" expresses direction. If there is 받침자음 except "ㄹ" in the last 음절, "~으로" is used. If there is no 받침자음 except "ㄹ", "~로" is used.

- [ ] 너의 집에/집으로 가거라.
Go to your home.

- [ ] 바닷가에/바닷가로 오너라.
Come to the beach.

- [ ] 그는 정원의 꽃에 물을 주었다.
He sprinkled the flower in the garden.

~에, ~부터 specification of time

- [ ] 나는 아침 여덟 시에 떠날 예정이다.
I'm going to leave at 8 o'clock in the morning.

- [ ] 내일 아침에 공항에서 만나자.
Let us see at the airport tomorrow morning.

- [ ] 우리는 이번 가을에 결혼할 예정이다.
We are going to marry this coming autumn.

"~부터" is for the exact starting time.

- [ ] 한국어 수업은 열 시에/시부터 시작한다.
The class of Korean starts at(from) 10 o'clock.

- [ ] 영어수업은 다섯 시에 끝난다.
The English class ends at 5 o'clock.

- [ ] 미사는 한 시간 후에 끝납니다.
The mass will be over 1 hour later, sir.

- [ ] 기차는 10분 전에 떠났다.
The train left 10 minutes ago.

~에게서, ~한테서, ~로부터 receding from human-being or animal

- [ ] 아버지에게서/아버지로부터/어버지한테서 용돈을 받았다.
I received pocket money from my father.

"~한테서" is more colloquial than others.

- [ ] 친구에게서/친구한테서/친구로부터 편지가 왔다.
A letter came from a friend.

- [ ] 그는 개한테서/개로부터/개에게서 멀리 달아났다.
He ran far away from the dog.

☐ 그 아이는 엄마에게서/엄마한테서/엄마로부터 멀어졌다.
The child moved away from the mother.

"~한테" is more colloquial than "~에게"

~에게, ~한테 approaching to human-being or animal(dative case)

☐ 개가 고양이한테/고양이에게 달려갔다.
The dog ran to the cat.

☐ 철수가 영자에게/영자한테 꽃을 선물했다.
Cheolsu presented flowers to Yeongja.

☐ 저는 아버님에게 용돈을 드렸습니다.
I gave my father some pocket money, sir.

☐ 미국은 우리에게 중요한 우방이다.
The United States is an important ally to us.

~와, ~과, ~(이)하고, ~(이)랑 together as partner or rival

☐ 우리는 어젯밤 적군과 싸웠다.
We fought the enemy last night.

☐ 저는 영미와 결혼하고 싶습니다.
I want to marry Yeongmi, sir.

☐ 영수는 석현이하고 수영을 하고 있다.
Yeongsu is swimming with Seokhyeon.

☐ 철수와 기택은 친구이다.
Cheolsu and Gitaek are friends.

"~(이)랑" is more colloquial than others.

☐ 나는 영선이랑 술래잡기를 했다.
I played hide-and-seek with Yeongseon.

☐ 나는 아침에 커피랑 빵을 먹는다.
I take coffee and bread in the morning.

☐ 바나나와 파인애플과 망고는 필리핀의 주요 과일이다.
Banana, pineapple and mango are the main fruits of the Philippines.

체언 which is suffixed with "~(으)로서" means the same entity as 주어, therefore "혜영" and "친구" are the same person.

체언 which is suffixed with "~(으)로" means the same entity as 목적어, therefore "영희" and "친구" are the same person.

~(으)로서, ~(으)로 — **qualification, status, social position**

- ☐ 혜영은 그를 친구로서 돕는다.
  Hyeyeong helps him as a friend.
- ☐ 그는 대통령으로서 임무를 수행하고 있다.
  He fulfills his role as President.
- ☐ 민오는 영희를 친한 친구로 생각한다.
  Mino thinks of Yeonghi as an intimate friend.
- ☐ 수미는 그를 남편으로 맞았다.
  Sumi accepted him as her husband.

~(으)로, ~(으)로써 — **instrument, method, material**

"~(으)로써" is used when emphasizing the volition or deed.

- ☐ 나는 비행기로 필리핀에 간다.
  I go to the Philippines by plane.
- ☐ 그는 빌린 돈으로 집을 샀다.
  He bought a house with a loan.
- ☐ 이 길로 가거라.
  Go this way.
- ☐ 그는 죽음으로/죽음으로써 공산주의에 반대했다.
  He opposed the communism by death.
- ☐ 그는 나무로 집을 지었다.
  Bread is made with flour, sir.
- ☐ 그는 감사의 뜻을 말로/말로써 표현하였다.
  He expressed his thanks in words.

~부터, ~까지, ~부터 ~까지, ~에서 ~까지 — **boundary, limit**

"~에서" and "~부터" can be used together for starting point of time and place, but when expressing time, if the starting time is not exact, "~에서" can not be used.

- ☐ 나부터 강을 건너겠다.
  I will cross the river first.
- ☐ 끝까지 최선을 다해라(←다하다).
  Do your best till the end.
- ☐ 학교부터/학교에서 너의 집까지 얼마나 멀어?
  How far is it from school to your house?

☐ 처음부터 중간까지 읽어라.
Read from the beginning to the middle.

☐ 저는 월요일부터/월요일에서 수요일까지 휴가입니다.
I'm on vacation from Monday to Wednesday, sir.

☐ 점심시간은 12시부터/12시에서 1시까지입니다.
Lunch time is from 12AM to 1PM, sir.

☐ 나는 작년부터 한국에서 살고 있다.
I have been living in Korea since last year.

☐ 1991년부터/1991년에서 1995년까지 나는 미국, 뉴저지에서 근무했다.
From 1991 to 1995 I worked in New Jersey, USA.

~(으)로, ~에	reason, cause

☐ 많은 사람이 암으로 죽는다.
Many people die of cancer.

☐ 폭우에/폭우로 집들이 떠내려갔다.
Houses were swept away by heavy rain.

☐ 태풍에/태풍으로 많은 나무가 쓰러졌다.
Many trees fell down due to typhoon.

☐ 나는 바람소리에 잠이 깼다.
Because of the noise of wind, I woke up.

~에	unit

☐ 나는 수박 한 통을 500원에 샀다.
I bought a watermelon for 500Won.

☐ 나는 한 달에 30만원을 임대료로 지불한다.
I pay 300,000Won a month as rent.

☐ 쌀 한 포대에 5만원이다.
One sack of rice is fifty thousand Won.

~(으)로	change, variation

☐ 물이 얼음으로 변했다.
The water has changed to ice.

☐ 임대료를 10만원에서 20만원으로 인상했다.
I raised the rent from 100,000Won to 200,000Won.

☐ 그는 사기꾼으로 알려졌다(← 알려지다).
He was known as a cheater.

☐ 뽕나무 밭이 바다로 변했다.
The mulberry field has changed to the sea.

"더" is 부사 which is used for the comparative degree.
많다./더 많다.: many(much)/more
빠르다./더 빠르다.: fast/faster

~보다	differential comparison

☐ 이 산은 저 산보다 (더) 높다.
This mountain is higher than that mountain.

☐ 영자는 순자보다 키가 (더) 크다.
Yeongja is taller than Sunja.

☐ 비행기는 기차보다 (더) 빠르다.
The plane is faster than the train.

~만큼, ~처럼	equivalent comparison

☐ 혜영이는 순희처럼/순희만큼 예쁘다.
Hyeyeoung is as pretty as Sunhee.

☐ 기호는 영철이처럼/영철이만큼 빨리 달린다.
Giho runs as fast as Yeongcheol.

☐ 오늘은 어제만큼/어제처럼 춥지 않다.
Today is not so cold as yesterday.

☐ 하늘만큼 땅만큼 널 사랑한다.
I love you as big as heaven and as big as earth.

~에서	circumstance, field, realm

☐ 이 세상에서 가장 아름다운 여자는 누구냐?
Who is the most beautiful woman in the world?

☐ 우리 사회에서 가장 어려운 문제는 지역감정이다.
The most difficult problem in our society is regional sentiment.

☐ 우리 반에서 영수가 제일 똑똑하다.
Yeongsu is the smartest in our class.

~라고	direct speech (직접화법)

☐ 동수는 "아빠, 저는 학교에 가요."라고 말했다.
Dongsu said, "I'm going to school, daddy."

☐ 그는 "도둑이야!"라고 소리쳤다.
He shouted, "Thief!".

☐ 경찰은 "그 사람 누구냐?"라고 물었다.
The police asked, "Who is he?"

~대로	accordance, pursuance

☐ 모든 것이 내 생각대로 되었다.
Everything was done as I thought.

☐ 저 아이는 무엇이든지 제멋대로 한다.
That boy does everything in his own way.

☐ 그들은 왕의 명령대로 행동했다.
They acted accordingly as the king ordered.

☐ 네 마음대로 해라.
It's up to you.

6 서술격조사 →Section 4, 7, 8, 10

Among the types of 조사, 서술격조사[~이다] is a quite unique 조사 because "~이다" is inflected according to the tense and the degrees of honorific like 용언.

7 호격조사 →Section 4(Vocative case)

8 부사격조사 for indirect speech(간접화법)

평서문 with 동사 or 형용사, 감탄문	~고

- [ ] 동수는 학교에 간다고 말했다./했다.
  Dongsu said that he was going to school.

- [ ] 민지는 빵을 먹겠다고 말했어요./했어요.
  Minji said that she would eat bread, Mr. ~.
- [ ] 그는 집이 정말 크다고 말했습니다./했습니다.
  He said that the house was really big, madam.

- [ ] 꽃이 매우 아름답다고 누나가 감탄했다.
  My sister exclaimed what a beautiful flower it was.

- [ ] 수미는 경치가 아름답다고 말했다./했다.
  Sumi said that the scenery was beautiful.

- [ ] 영수는 착하다고 선생님께서 칭찬하셨다.
  The teacher praised that Yeongsu is good-natured.

평서문 with 서술격조사	~(이)라고

- [ ] 그는 직업이 군인이라고 썼다.
  He wrote that his occupation was a soldier.

- [ ] 순미는 학생이라고 말했다.
  Sunmi said she was a student.

- [ ] 자기는 도둑이 아니라고 철호가 주장했다.
  Cheolho insisted that he was not a thief.

- [ ] 민호는 교사가 아니라고 아버지가 말씀하셨다.
  Father said Minho was not a teacher.

의문문	~(이)냐고

- [ ] 아버지께서 왜 나가냐고 물으셨다(← 묻다).
  asked why I was going out.

☐ 엄마가 뭐 먹냐고 물었어요.
Mom asked me what I was eating, daddy.

☐ 경찰은 직업이 무엇이냐고 물었다.
The police asked me what my job was.

☐ 수업이 재미있냐고 선생님이 질문하셨다.
The teacher asked if the class was interesting.

명령문	~(으)라고

☐ 사장님이 내일부터 출근하라고 말했습니다./했습니다.
Boss told me to come to work from tomorrow, sir.

☐ 선생님이 더 열심히 공부하라고 말씀하셨다./하셨다.
The teacher told me to study harder.

☐ 장군은 적의 공격을 막으라고(←막다) 명령했다.
The general ordered to defend the attack of enemy.

청유문	~자고

☐ 영희가 영화를 보자고 말했다./했다.
Yeonghi asked me to see a movie.

☐ 아내가 한국에서 살자고 말했어요./했어요.
My wife said that we live in Korea, Mr. ~.

* "~고 말하다." and "~고 하다." have the same meaning as "say that ~".
* "~고 말씀하셨다./하셨다." is 과거시제 of "~고 말씀하시다./하시다." which is 높임표현.

- Colloquial expressions in 간접화법
  ① (용언)~대요./~답니다.
  - 동수는 학교에 간다고 말했어요./말했습니다.
    → 동수는 학교에 간대요./간답니다.
  - 민지는 빵을 먹겠다고 말했어요./말했습니다.
    → 민지는 빵을 먹겠대요./먹겠답니다.
  - 그는 집이 정말 크다고 말했어요./말했습니다.
    → 그는 집이 정말 크대요./크답니다.

• 수미는 경치가 아름답다고 말했어요./말했습니다.
→ 수미는 경치가 아름답대요./아름답답니다.

② (서술격조사)~(이)래요./~(이)랍니다.

• 순미는 학생이라고 말했어요./말했습니다.
→ 순미는 학생이래요./학생이랍니다.
• 민호는 선생이 아니라고 말했어요./말했습니다.
→ 민호는 선생이 아니래요./아니랍니다.
• 그는 직업이 군인이라고(교사라고) 말했어요./말했습니다.
→ 그는 직업이 군인이래요.(교사래요.)/군인이랍니다.(교사랍니다.)

③ (동사 in 청유문)~재요./~잡니다.

• 영희가 영화를 보자고 말했어요./말했습니다.
→ 영희가 영화를 보재요./보잡니다.
• 아내가 한국에서 살자고 말했어요./말했습니다.
→ 아내가 한국에서 살재요./살잡니다.

* If "요" from "~대요.", "~(이)래요." and "~재요." are omitted, the sentences change to 반말.

2. 보조사

보조사 expresses the attitude or opinion of the person speaking by additional meaning to 체언 instead of 격조사 or with 격조사 together. Therefore, 보조사 cannot be omitted due to the additional meaning.

~은, ~는	comparison, contrast, description for subject

☐ 밤은 어둡고, 낮은 밝다.
The night is dark and the day is bright.

☐ 저는 필리핀에서 온 마틴 후안이라고 합니다.
I'm Juan Martin from the Philippines, sir.

☐ 저는 그것이 좋은 방법이라고 생각합니다.
I think that's a good way, sir.

□ 고래는 물고기가 아니다.
The whale is not a fish.

□ 그 바나나는 영수가 먹었다.
That banana was eaten by Yeongsu.

□ 오늘 회의의 주제는 한국의 미래입니다.
The topic of today's meeting is the future of Korea, gentlemen.

~밖에	exception

"~밖에" is always followed by the negative 서술어.

□ 그는 우리 반에서 명숙이밖에 좋아하지 않는다.
He doesn't like anyone in our class except Myeongsuk.

□ 나는 만원밖에 없다.
I have no money except ten thousand Won.

□ 나는 너밖에 모른다.
I don't know anyone but you.

~만, ~뿐(이다.)	uniqueness, exclusivity, limitation

"~만" and "뿐": symmetrical meaning to "~밖에"

□ 나는 너만 믿는다.
I trust only you.

□ 나만 오늘 학교에 갔다.
Only I went to school today.

□ 그가 좋아하는 학생은 지민이뿐이다.
His favorite student is only Jimin.

□ 믿을 사람은 너뿐이다.
I have no one but you to rely upon.

~마다	all, every

- 날마다: every day
- 이틀마다: every other day
- 집집마다: from house to house, every house
- 곳곳마다: everywhere
- 갈 적마다: every time one goes

□ 너를 볼 때마다 너의 아버지가 생각난다.
Every time I see you, I think of your father.

☐ 사람마다 그를 칭찬한다.
Everybody praises him.

☐ 버스는 5분마다 떠난다.
The buses start every five minutes.

~도, ~조차, ~마저, ~까지	belonging inclusion, together

"~조차" and "~마저" are for the negative situation in general.

☐ 나뿐만 아니라 정국이도 노래를 잘해요.
Not only me but Jeongguk also sings well, sir.

☐ 영만이조차/마저/까지/도 학교에 오지 않았다.
Yeongman also didn't come to school.

☐ 이런 것까지/것도 사오셨어요?
Did you buy this too, sir?

☐ 그 사람은 만나기조차 힘들다.
It's difficult even only to see him.

~(이)라도	consession

☐ 돈이 없으면, 구걸이라도 해라.
If you have no money, even beg.

☐ 어린애라도 그것을 안다.
Even a child knows it.

~(이)거나, ~(이)든 ~(이)든지, ~(이)든가	any ~, whatever

"~든" is 준말 of "~든지" or "~든가".

☐ 택시거나(~든/~든지/~든가) 버스거나(~든/~든지/~든가) 아무거나 타자.
Let's take a taxi or a bus or anything.

☐ 사과든(~든지/~거나/~든가) 귤이든(~이든지/~이거나/~이든가) 배든(~든지/~거나/~든가) 뭐든(=무엇이든) 좋아한다.
Apple or orange or pear, I like whatever.

☐ 돈이든가(~이든/~이거나/~이든지) 쌀이든가(~이든/~이거나/~이든지) 뭐든지(=무엇이든지) 너에게 주겠다.
I will give you money or rice or whatever.

~(이)라고	named, called

- [ ] 존이라고 하는 사람
  a man named/called John

- [ ] 그 당시 한국을 고려라고 불렀다.
  They called Korea "Koryŏ" at that time.

- [ ] 자네가 가는 곳이 어디라고 했나?
  Where did you say you are going?

~들	plural subject

"~들" is attached to 부사, 명사, 대명사 or derived words from 용언 to imply that 주어 of sentence is plural.

- [ ] 울지들 마라.
  Don't cry!

- [ ] 벌써 다들 떠났다.
  All of them have left.

- [ ] 많이들 먹어라.
  Eat a lot!

- [ ] 어서들 오세요.
  Welcome, gentlemen!

- [ ] 빨리들 가거라.
  Go quickly!

- [ ] 식사들 하셨습니까?
  Did you eat, sirs?

- [ ] 어서 밥들 먹어라.
  Come on and eat!

- [ ] 결혼들은 했을까?
  Did they get married?

2 Examples using 보조사 together with 격조사

- ☐ 사람은 빵만으로(만+으로) 살수 없다.
  Man cannot live on bread alone.

- ☐ 나에게는(에게+는) 명예가 가장 중요하다.
  Honor is the most important to me indeed.

- ☐ 정국이는 왼손으로도(으로+도) 글씨를 잘 쓴다.
  Jeongkuk writes well even with his left hand.

- ☐ 내 강아지는 방안에서만(에서+만) 잘 논다.
  My puppy plays well only in the room.

- ☐ 나는 서울로는(로+는) 안 간다.
  I'll not go to Seoul anyway.

- ☐ 공산주의 국가에서는(에서+는) 자유가 없다.
  In communist countries there is no freedom.

SECTION

16

용언 I : 동사

Declinable Word I: Verb

용언 which describes 주어 or 목적어 in detail by inflection of it's 어미 has two 품사(동사, 형용사) as 서술어. In addition, 서술격조사 is also used like 용언. The inflection of 어미(어미변화) for 용언 is explained in Section 21 and 22 in detail.

In 한국어, 동사 and 형용사 are very similar in function, so there is a saying that 형용사 is a part of 동사, or 동사 and 형용사 are siblings. Therefore, the rules of conjugation only for 동사 in 영어 are applied also to 형용사 in 한국어.

- Basic differences between 동사 and 형용사

구분	동사 (예: 가다/go, 먹다/eat, 공부하다/study)	형용사 (예: 아름답다/beautiful, 바쁘다 /busy, 검다/black, 시원하다/cool)
어미 for 현재시제	~ㄴ다./~는다. (간다. 먹는다. 공부한다.)	No change. (아름답다. 바쁘다. 검다. 시원하다.)
When used as 관형사 for 현재시제,	~는 (가는, 먹는, 공부하는)	~ㄴ/~은 (아름다운, 바쁜, 검은, 시원한)
Exclamatory 어미 for 현재시제,	~는구나! (가는구나! 먹는구나! 공부하는구나!)	~구나! (아름답구나! 바쁘구나! 검구나! 시원하구나!)
When "~아라/~어라" is used in 어미,	Imperative [가거라. 먹어라. 공부해(← 하여)라.]	Exclamatory [아름다워라! 바빠라! 검어라! 시원해(← 하여)라!]

동사 as 서술어 describes the action of 주어 and is divided into 규칙동사 and 불규칙동사 based on the type of inflection in 어간 and 어미. In this section, 규칙동사, 불규칙동사, 보조동사 and 파생동사 will be explained.

1. 규칙동사

• Case 1: There is no change in 어간 on any routine conjugation and 어미변화.

• Case 2: Even changed, it can be explained by the common rule which is applicable to all other same type of 동사.

1 No change in 어간[예: 읽다 → 읽(어간) + 다(어미)]

□ 나는 책을 읽는다.
I read a book.

□ 너는 이 책을 읽었느냐?
Did you read this book?

□ 우리 책을 읽자.
Let us read book.

□ 너는 책을 매우 잘 읽는구나!
You read book excellently!

* 동사 such as "읽다" which has no change in 어간 on the routine conjugation and 어미변화 is classified as 규칙동사.

* Other 규칙동사 of same type

• 입다: wear
• 먹다: eat
• 자다: sleep
• 씻다: wash
• 당기다: pull
• 벗다: remove clothes
• 닫다: close
• 믿다: believe
• 잡다: catch, hold
• 쏟다: pour
• 뛰다, 달리다: run
• 속다: be cheated
• 잊다: forget
• 씹다: chew
• 빼앗다: rob, take by force
• 묻다: bury
• 뽑다: pull out, root up

2 Omission of "ㄹ" from 어간[예: 얼다 → 얼(어간) + 다(어미)]

- 물이 언다.
  The water freezes.

- 물이 어느냐?
  Does the water freezes?

- 물이 얼고 있느냐?
  Is the water freezing?

- 물이 어는구나!
  The water is freezing!

- 물이 얼었습니다.
  The water is frozen, sir.

- 겨울에는 강이 업니다.
  The river freezes in winter, sir.

* "ㄹ" of 어간 is changed by the routine conjugation and 어미변화 like "언다." for 현재시제 and omitted by the common rule that the initial consonant of the following 음절 is "ㄴ" like "~는구나!" or that 어간 is combined to "~ㅂ니다." for 높임표현. Because the change and omission of "ㄹ" from "얼다" is based on the common rule for all of "~ㄹ다"-동사, "얼다" is classified as 규칙동사.

* Other 규칙동사 of same type

- 울다: cry
- 돌다: turn, go round
- 열다: open
- 알다: know
- 썰다: slice, cut up
- 갈다: grind
- 몰다: drive
- 달다: hang, put up
- 밀다: push

3 Omission of "으" from 어간(예: 쓰다)

- 편지는 연필로 쓰세요.
  Please, write a letter with a pencil, Mr. ~!

- 펜으로 쓰면 지울 수 없어요.
  If you write with a pen, you can't erase it, Miss ~.

- [ ] 나는 친구에게 편지를 써(← 쓰어)서 우체통에 넣었다.
  I wrote a letter to a friend and put it in the mailbox.

- [ ] 부모님께 문안편지를 썼(← 쓰었)다.
  I wrote a letter to my parents to say hello.

- [ ] 지금 즉시 형에게 편지를 써(← 쓰어)라.
  Write to the brother right now.

* "으" in 어간 of "쓰다" is omitted and changed to "어" by the common rule that the following 음절 has a medial vowel(중간모음) which are "어" and "었".

* Other 규칙동사 of same type

- 따르다: follow, pour
- 뜨다: float, rise(sun, moon)
- 담그다: soak
- 크다: grow (up)
- 치르다: pay
- 끄다: extinguish, turn off
- 잠그다: lock

2. 불규칙동사

When a 동사 has change in 어간 or 어미, while the others which have the same type of 동사 have no change as 규칙동사, this 동사 is classified as 불규칙동사. Among 11 types of 불규칙동사(ㄷ, ㄹ, ㅂ, ㅅ, 으, 우, 르, 러, 여, 거라, 너라), 7 typical types will be explained here in detail.

1 어간-불규칙동사

1 ㅅ-불규칙동사(예: 짓다)

- [ ] 나는 집을 짓는다.
  I'm building a house.

- [ ] 나는 집을 지었습니다.
  I built a house, sir.

☐ 여기에 집을 지으면 더 좋겠다.
It would be better if we build a house here.

☐ 나는 집을 짓고 아내는 아이를 돌본다.
I build a house and my wife takes care of the child.

* "ㅅ" in 어간 of "짓다" is omitted when the following 음절 has 중간모음. But in other "~ㅅ다"-동사(예: 벗다, 씻다), "ㅅ" is not omitted on any conjugation and 어미변화. Therefore, "짓다" is classified as ㅅ-불규칙동사.

* Other 불규칙동사 of same type

- 낫다: get well, heal
- 붓다: pour, swell up
- 잇다: connect, join
- 긋다: draw (a line)
- 젓다: stir, paddle

2 ㄷ-불규칙동사(예: 묻다)

☐ 수미가 가격을 묻는다.
Sumi asks about the price.

☐ 수미가 가격을 물었다.
Sumi asked about the price.

☐ 수미가 가격을 묻습니다.
Sumi asks about the price, sir.

☐ 수미가 가격을 물으면 점원이 대답한다.
If Sumi asks the price, the clerk answers.

* "ㄷ" in 어간 of "묻다" changes to "ㄹ" when the following 음절 has 중간모음. But in other "~ㄷ다" 동사(예: 닫다, 쏟다), "ㄷ" does not change on any conjugation and 어미변화.

* Other 불규칙동사 of same type

- 걷다: walk
- 깨닫다: realize, understand
- 듣다: listen
- 싣다: load

3 르-불규칙동사(예: 모르다)

☐ 해수는 그 사건을 모른다.
Haesu doesn't know the happening.

☐ 나는 모르지만 해수는 안다.
I don't know but Haesu knows.

☐ 나는 몰랐(← 모르았)고 해수는 알고 있었다.
I didn't know but Haesu knew.

☐ 저는 그것을 모릅니다./몰라(← 모르아)요.
I don't know, sir./auntie.

☐ 저는 그것을 몰랐습니다.
I didn't know that, sir.

☐ 나는 이것을 몰라도 너는 이것을 알아야 한다.
Even though I don't know this, you should know this.

* "모르" changes to "몰ㄹ~" when the following 음절 has 중간모음, while other "~르다"-동사(치르다/pay, 따르다/follow) does not change as 규칙동사.

* Other 불규칙동사 of same type

- 가르다: divide
- 기르다: raise, bring up
- 누르다: press
- 찌르다: stab, prick
- 머무르다: stay
- 고르다: select
- 나르다: carry, transport
- 오르다: go up, ascend
- 흐르다: flow, stream

4 ㅂ-불규칙동사(예: 돕다)

☐ 나는 아픈 사람을 돕는다.
I help the sick person.

☐ 너희들은 서로 도와야 한다.
You must help each other.

☐ 나는 그를 도왔습니다.
I helped him, sir.

☐ 나는 지금 아내를 돕고 있다.
I am helping my wife now.

☐ 가난한 사람을 도우면, 복을 받을 것이다.
If you help the poor, you will be blessed.

* "ㅂ" from "돕" is omitted when the following 음절 has 중간모음.
In other "~ㅂ다"-동사(입다/wear, 씹다/chew), "ㅂ" is not omitted.
Therefore, "돕다" is classified as 불규칙동사.

* Other 불규칙동사 of same type

- 굽다: roast, broil, bake
- 눕다: lie down
- 줍다: pick up

2 어미-불규칙동사

1 여–불규칙동사[예: 공부하다 → 공부하(어간)+다(어미)]

☐ 나는 영어를 공부한다.
I study English.

☐ 수영이는 공부하고 영수는 잠을 잔다.
Suyeong is studying and Yeongsu is sleeping.

☐ 수영이는 열심히 공부해(← 하여)서 대학교에 입학했다.
Suyoung studied hard and entered college.

☐ 오늘은 학교에서 수학을 공부했(← 하였)습니다.
Today I studied mathematics in the school, sir.

☐ 영수는 열심히 공부해(← 하여)도 시험성적이 안 좋다.
Even though Yeongsu studies hard, the test results are not good.

* While 어미 of ordinary 동사 changes to "~아/어", "~아도/어도", "~아서/어서", "~았/었~", etc. on conjugation and 어미변화, but 어미 of "~하다"-동사 changes to "~여", "~여도", "~여서", "~였~", etc. Therefore, all "~하다"-동사 are classified as 여-불규칙동사. "~해/했~" is the abbreviation from "~하여/하였~" and used commonly.

* Other 불규칙동사 of same type

- 등산하다: climb the mountain
- 생각하다: think
- 일하다: work
- 원하다: want, wish

2 거라-불규칙동사

For the imperative mood in 반말, 어미(~다) of 동사 changes normally to "~아라./~어라." But "가다(go)" and "자다(sleep) change to "가거라." and "자거라.".

돌아가다
돌다/turn + 가다/go

올라가다
오르다/climb, ascend + 가다

- ☐ 지금 즉시 집으로 가거라.
  Go home right now.
- ☐ 학교로 돌아가거라.
  Go back to school./Return to school.
- ☐ 지붕에 올라가거라.
  Go up to the roof.
- ☐ 소파에서 자지 말고, 침대에서 자거라.
  Don't sleep on the sofa, sleep on the bed.

3 너라-불규칙동사(오다/come)

너라-불규칙동사 is the same case as 거라-불규칙동사.

- ☐ 지금 즉시 집으로 오너라.
  Come home right now.
- ☐ 학교로 돌아오너라.
  Come back to school./Return to school.
- ☐ 지붕에 올라오너라.
  Come up to the roof.

3. 보조동사

보조동사 is placed behind the main 동사 or 형용사 and adds additional meaning. Mostly 보조동사 follows 동사 except some cases that it follows 형용사.

~지 않는다, ~지 못하다, ~지 말다	denial, negation

→ Section 10

~게 하다	assignment, causation

☐ 나는 거기에 집을 짓게(← 짓다) 했다.
I had a house built there.

☐ 그는 개한테 생선을 먹게(← 먹다) 했다.
He let the dog eat fish.

~아/어 지다	passiveness

☐ 이렇게 하면 홍수가 막아(← 막다) 진다.
If you do in this way, the flood will be protected.

☐ 이 공장에서 자동차가 만들어(← 만들다) 집니다.
Cars are made in this factory, sir.

~게 되다	change, transformation

☐ 공산주의에서는 자유를 잃게(← 잃다) 된다.
In communism the freedom comes to be lost.

☐ 운동을 안 하면 살이 찌게(← 찌다) 된다.
If you do not exercise, you will gain weight.

~아/어 오다	coming progress

☐ 날이 점점 밝아(← 밝다) 온다.
Gradually the day is getting brighter.

☐ 떠날 날이 가까워(← 가깝다) 왔다.
The day to leave has come near.

☐ 영수가 뛰어(← 뛰다) 온다.
Yeongsu comes running.

~아/어 가다	receding progress

점점 as 부사 means "by degrees, little by little, gradually, more and more, etc".

☐ 환자가 죽어(← 죽다) 간다.
The patient is dying.

☐ 그는 나에게서 점점 멀어져(← 멀어지다) 갔다.
He went away from me further and further.

~고 나다 (~고 나서 ~)	afterwards

☐ 샤워를 하고(← 하다) 나서 식사를 했다.
I ate after taking a shower.

☐ 아침을 먹고(← 먹다) 나서 학교에 갔다.
After eating breakfast I went to school.

~고 있다 →Section 7	progressive of attitude or situation

☐ 그는 신문을 읽고(← 읽다) 있었다.
He was reading a newspaper.

☐ 그는 운동장을 달리고(← 달리다) 있습니다.
He is running on the playground, sir.

~아/어 버리다	complete termination

☐ 버스에서 지갑을 잃어(← 잃다) 버렸다.
I lost away my purse on the bus.

☐ 개가 생선을 먹어(← 먹다) 버렸다.
The dog ate up the fish.

☐ 나는 이미 그 책을 읽어(← 읽다) 버렸다.
I read through the book already.

~아/어 주다	service, offer

☐ 아들에게 자전거를 사(← 사다) 주었다.
I bought a bicycle for my son.

☐ 딸에게 인형을 만들어(← 만들다) 주었다.
I made a doll for my daughter.

~아/어 드리다	service, offer

☐ 나는 할아버지에게 밥을 지어(←짓다) 드렸다.
I cooked a meal for my grandfather.

Humble expression
→ Section 8

☐ 나는 할머니에게 돋보기를 사(←사다) 드렸다.
I bought a magnifying glass for my grandmother.

~아/어 보다	attempt, trial

☐ 아버님, 이것 좀 드셔(←드시어←드시다) 보세요.
Dad, please taste it.

☐ 나는 얼음을 만져(←만지어←만지다) 보았다.
I touched and felt the ice.

~아/어 대다	overstatement

☐ 강당에 있는 모든 사람들이 함께 웃어(←웃다) 대었다.
Everyone in the hall laughed out loud.

☐ 그는 큰 소리로 내 이름을 불러(←부르다) 대었다.
He called my name out loud.

~아야/어야 한다	duty, obligation

☐ 너는 이 약을 먹어야(←먹다) 한다.
You must take this medicine.

☐ 아이들은 학교에서 공부해야(←공부하다) 한다.
Children should study in the school.

~ㄹ 수 있다	ability

☐ 나는 자전거를 탈(←타다) 수 있다.
I can ride a bicycle.

☐ 영호는 영어로 말할(←말하다) 수 있다.
Youngho can speak in English.

~기는 하다	concession

- [ ] 나는 그 사람을 만나기는(←만나다) 했다.
I admit that I met that person.

- [ ] 그는 순남이를 좋아하기는(←좋아하다) 했다고 인정했다.
He conceded that he liked Sunnam.

~ㄴ/는 척하다, ~ㄴ/는 체하다	pretense, feint

- [ ] 그는 아픈(←아프다) 척하고/체하고 얼굴을 찡그리고 있다.
He is frowning for pretending to be sick.

- [ ] 자는(←자다) 척하지/체하지 마.
Don't pretend to sleep!

~아/어 놓다	retention, keeping

- [ ] 더워서 나는 창문을 열어(←열다) 놓았다.
Because it was hot, I left the window open.

- [ ] 나는 옷을 못에 걸어(←걸다) 놓았다.
I kept my clothes hung on the nail.

~아/어 두다	retention, keeping

- [ ] 나는 돈을 책상서랍에 넣어(←넣다) 두었다.
I kept money in the desk drawer.

- [ ] 내 말을 잘 들어(←듣다) 둬(←두다).
Listen well and remember what I say.

~아/어 보이다	show, demonstration

- [ ] 그는 나에게 글자를 써(←쓰어←쓰다) 보였다.
He wrote letters and showed me.

- [ ] 엄마는 아기에게 방긋 웃어(←웃다) 보였어요.
Mom smiled beautifully at her baby, Mr. ~.

4. 파생동사

1 명사 + "~하다"

By adding suffix(접미사) of "~하다" to 명사 which implies the meaning of act, feeling or change as 어근(word-root), 동사 is derived.

- 공부하다: study
- 성공하다: succeed
- 금지하다: forbid, prohibit
- 수정하다: correct
- 결혼하다: marry
- 출산하다: give birth to
- 사랑하다: love
- 수영하다: swim

☐ 그들은 어제 교회에서 결혼했다.
They were married in church yesterday.

☐ 이 호수는 낚시를 금지하고 있다.
This lake is forbidden to fish.

2 어간 of 형용사 + "~아/어하다" → Transitive verb(타동사)

- 밉다: hateful → 미워하다: hate
- 기쁘다: glad → 기뻐하다: be glad of
- 창피하다: shameful → 창피해하다: feel shame about
- 귀엽다: cute → 귀여워하다: make a pet of, love
- 미안하다: sorry → 미안해하다: feel sorry about
- 고맙다: thankful → 고마워하다: thank for

☐ 할머니는 손녀를 매우 귀여워하신다.
Grandma loves her granddaughter so much.

☐ 철수는 자기의 잘못을 미안해한다.
Cheolsu feels sorry for his mistake.

☐ 먼저 아내에게 고마워하고 싶다.
I want to thank my wife first.

"~고 싶다" is 보조형용사.
→ Section 17

3 어간 of 형용사 + "~아/어지다" → Intransitive verb(자동사)

- 높다: high → 높아지다: become higher, rise
- 크다:big, large → 커지다: grow bigger/larger
- 예쁘다: pretty, beautiful → 예뻐지다: become pretty/beautiful
- 낮다: low → 낮아지다: come to be lower
- 귀엽다: cute → 귀여워지다: get cute
- 좋다: good → 좋아지다: get better
- 나쁘다: bad → 나빠지다: get worse
- 밝다: bright → 밝아지다: brighten
- 검다: black → 검어지다: become black

☐ 가을에는 하늘이 높아진다.
In autumn the sky gets higher.

☐ 아기가 점점 더 귀여워진다.
Baby keeps getting cuter and cuter.

☐ 경제가 좋아지고 있다.
The economy is getting better.

4 Echoic or mimetic adverbs→Section 18 + "~(이)다/~대다/~거리다" → 자동사

- 찰랑찰랑 → 찰랑이다/찰랑거리다/찰랑대다: To lap with ripple such as a small wave in a pool
- 출렁출렁 → 출렁이다/출렁거리다/출렁대다: To undulate such as a wave in the sea
- 펄럭펄럭 → 펄럭이다/펄럭거리다/펄럭대다: To flutter in the wind such as a big flag
- 팔락팔락 → 팔락이다/팔락거리다: To flap in the wind such as a small flag or falling leaves
- 컹컹 → 컹컹대다/컹컹거리다: To keep barking
- 흔들흔들 → 흔들거리다: To sway
- 살랑살랑 → 살랑이다/살랑대다/살랑거리다: To move gently, to walk lightly or to blow softly

☐ 파도가 심하게 출렁댄다.
Waves are undulating violently.

☐ 태극기가 바람에 펄럭인다.
The Korean national flag is fluttering in the wind.

☐ 이웃집 개가 밤새 컹컹거렸다.
The neighbor's dog was barking all night.

☐ 가을 바람이 살랑거린다.
An autumn breeze blows softly.

SECTION

17

용언 II: 형용사

Declinable Word II: Adjective

형용사 as 서술어 describes the attribute and the situation about 주어 and also is divided into 규칙형용사 and 불규칙형용사 like 동사. 규칙형용사, 불규칙형용사, 보조형용사 and 파생형용사 will be explained here.

1. 규칙형용사

규칙형용사 has the same rules as 규칙동사.

1 No change in 어간[예: 싫다 → 싫(어간) + 다(어미)]

- [ ] 나는 갑제가 싫다.
I dislike Gapje.

- [ ] 갑제는 싫지만 영호는 좋다.
I dislike Gapje but I like Yeongho.

- [ ] 어렸을 때 갑제가 정말 싫었다.
I really disliked Gapje when I was young.

* There is no change in 어간 on the routine conjugation and 어미변화.
* Other 규칙형용사 of same type

- 짧다: short
- 넓다: wide
- 밝다: bright
- 검다: black
- 희다: white
- 굵다: thick
- 좁다: narrow

2 Omission of "ㄹ" from 어간[예: 길다 → 길(어간) + 다(어미)]

- [ ] 머리카락이 길다.
The hair is long.

- [ ] 머리카락이 길어서/기니까 불편하다.
It is uncomfortable because the hair is long.

- [ ] 머리카락이 기네요.
The hair is long, Miss ~.

- [ ] 머리카락이 긴 사람은 들어올 수 없습니다.
People with long hair cannot enter, sir.

- [ ] 저의 머리카락은 깁니다.
My hair is long, sir.

☐ 머리카락이 길면 이발소에 가거라.
If you have long hair, go to a barber shop.

* "ㄹ" from 어간 is omitted when the following 음절 has "ㄴ" as the initial consonant or changes to another 받침자음(긴, 깁) according to the common rule for all "~ㄹ다"-형용사. Therefore, "길다" is classified as 규칙형용사.

* Other 규칙형용사 of same type

- 멀다: faraway
- 달다: sweet
- 둥글다: round
- 어질다: kindhearted

3 Omission of "으" from 어간[예: 아프다 → 아프(어간) + 다(어미)]

☐ 머리가 아픕니다./아파(← 프아)요.
I have headache, sir./Mr. ~.

☐ 머리가 아프니까/아파(← 프아)서 잠을 못 자요.
I can not sleep because of headache, Mr. ~.

☐ 머리가 아프면 약을 먹어라.
If you have a headache, take medicine!

☐ 어제는 머리가 아팠(← 프았)다.
I had a headache yesterday.

* "으" of all "~으다"-형용사 in 어간 is omitted by the common rule that the following 음절 has 중간모음.

* Other 규칙형용사 of same type

- 고프다: hungry
- 기쁘다: glad
- 바쁘다: busy
- 슬프다: sad
- 아프다: painful
- 쓰다: bitter
- 크다: big, tall

2. 불규칙형용사

Among 8 types of 불규칙형용사(ㄹ, ㅂ, ㅅ, 으, 르, 러, ㅎ, 여),
6 typical types will be explained here in detail.

1 어간-불규칙형용사

1 ㅅ-불규칙형용사(예: 낫다)

- 이 회사는 저 회사보다 낫습니다,/나아요.
  This company is better than that company, sir./Mr. ~.
- 어렸을 때 경수는 나보다 나았다.
  When young, Gyeongsu was better than me.
- 아들의 인생은 아버지의 인생보다 나아야 한다.
  The life of son must be better than the life of father.

* "ㅅ" from 어간 is omitted when the following 음절 has 중간모음.

2 ㅂ-불규칙형용사(예: 쉽다)

- 이 문제는 너무 쉬워(← 우어)요./쉽습니다.
  This problem is too easy, Mr. ~./sir.
- 이 문제는 쉬워도 저 문제는 쉽지 않다.
  This problem is easy, but that problem is not easy.
- 문제들이 더 쉬우면 좋겠다.
  I hope the problems are easier.
- 이 문제는 쉽지만 푸는데(← 풀다) 오래 걸린다.
  This problem is easy but takes a long time to solve.
- 어제 시험은 쉬웠(← 우었)다.
  Yesterday's exam was easy.

* "ㅂ" changes to "~우~" when the following 음절 has 중간모음(어, 었).
  But in other "~ㅂ다"-형용사(예: 좁다/narrow), "좁" does not change
  as 규칙형용사.

* Other 불규칙형용사 of same type

- 맵다: hot, pungent
- 덥다: hot
- 춥다: cold
- 가깝다: near
- 바보스럽다: stupid
- 아름답다: beautiful
- 어렵다: difficult
- 즐겁다: joyful, merry
- 자비롭다: merciful
- 곱다: pretty, lovely, tender

3 르-불규칙형용사(예: 다르다)

☐ 이것은 그것과 다르다.
This is different from that.

☐ 영수는 영철이와 많이 달라(← 다르아)요./다릅니다.
Youngsu is very different from Youngchul, uncle./sir.

☐ 우리는 성격이 달라서 자주 싸운다.
We fight often because we have different characters.

☐ 이 가격도 다르지 않다.
This price is not different too.

☐ 그들은 성격이 너무 달랐(← 다르았)습니다./달랐어요.
Their characters were so different, sir./Mr. ~.

* "다르" of 어간 changes to "달ㄹ~" when the following 음절 has 중간모음(아, 았).

* Other 불규칙형용사 of same type

- 빠르다: fast. quick
- 게으르다: lazy
- 이르다: early
- 서투르다: unskillful, awkward

* "~르다"-형용사 is 르-불규칙형용사 or 러-불규칙형용사.

2 어미-불규칙형용사

1 여-불규칙형용사[예: 행복하다 → 행복하(어간) + 다(어미)]

☐ 나의 어머니는 행복하시다.
My mother is happy.

☐ 아내는 행복해(← 하여)서 눈물을 흘렸다.
My wife shed tears because she was happy.

- ☐ 수영이는 대학교에 입학해(← 하여)서 행복했(← 하였)다.
  Suyoung was happy because she entered the university.

- ☐ 영희는 행복하지만/행복해도 수영이는 행복하지 않다.
  Yeonghi is happy but Suyeong is not happy.

* 여-불규칙형용사 is the same case as 여-불규칙동사.

* Other 불규칙형용사 of same type

- 깨끗하다: clean
- 시원하다: cool
- 피곤하다: tired
- 조용하다: quiet

2 러-불규칙형용사[예: 푸르다 → 푸르(어간) + 다(어미)]

- ☐ 하늘은 푸르고 바람은 시원하다.
  The sky is blue and the wind is cool.

- ☐ 하늘이 푸르니까/푸르러(← 푸르어)서 경치가 더 아름답다.
  Because the sky is blue, the scenery is more beautiful.

- ☐ 하늘은 푸르러도 내 마음은 우울하다.
  Even though the sky is blue, but my heart is depressed.

- ☐ 어제는 하늘이 정말 푸르렀습니다.
  The sky was really blue yesterday, sir.

* 선어말어미 of "러/렀" is added to 어간 of "푸르" when the following 음절 has 중간모음(어, 었).

* Other 불규칙형용사 of same type.

- 누르다: yellowish brown

3 어간 and 어미-불규칙형용사

1 ㅎ-불규칙형용사[예: 하얗다 → 하얗(어간) + 다(어미)]

- ☐ 눈은 하얗다.
  The snow is white.

- ☐ 눈은 하얗고 가볍다.
  The snow is white and light.

□ 눈이 하얘(← 하얗아)요./눈이 하얗습니다.
The snow is white, daddy./sir.

□ 눈은 하얬(← 하얗았)어요./눈은 하얬습니다.
The snow was white, auntie./madam.

□ 눈이 하야(← 하얗으)니까/하얘(← 하얗아)서 아름답다.
The snow is beautiful because it is white.

* "ㅎ-받침자음" from "하얗" is omitted and changes to "~얘/얬~" when the following 음절 has 중간모음(으, 아, 았).
* Other 불규칙형용사 of same type(All of "~ㅎ다"-형용사 except "좋다"/good)

- 까맣다: coal-black
- 그렇다: so, that way
- 동그랗다: round
- 파랗다: blue, azure

3. 보조형용사

보조형용사 behind 용언 adds extra meaning. In case that 보조형용사 is the same as 보조동사, it means that the precedent word is 형용사.

~고 싶다	wish, desire

□ 나는 매운 라면이 먹고(← 먹다) 싶다.
I want to eat a pungent ramyon.

□ 나는 내일 너를 만나고(← 만나다) 싶다.
I hope to see you tomorrow.

~ㅆ으면 싶다	probable hope

□ 네가 시험에 합격했으면(← 합격하다) 싶다.
I wish that you pass the examination.

□ 이 소식이 사실이었으면(← 사실이다) 싶다.
I wish that this information is true.

~지 않다	negation, denial

☐ 이 꽃은 저 꽃만큼 아름답지(← 아름답다) 않다.
This flower is not so beautiful as that flower.

☐ 물이 맑지(← 맑다) 않다.
The water is not clear.

~지 못하다	deficiency, lack

☐ 물이 맑지 못하다.
The water is deficient in clarity.

☐ 그는 유능하지(← 유능하다) 못하다.
He is lacking in ability.

~기는 하다	concession

☐ 그것이 비싸지 않기는(← 비싸지 않다) 하다.
I admit that it's not expensive.

☐ 이 망고는 달기는(← 달다) 하다.
I agree that this mango is sweet.

~나 보다, ~ㄴ가 보다, ~는가 보다, ~ㄹ까 하다	guess, estimation

☐ 태풍이 오나/오는가(← 오다) 보다.
It's seems that a storm is coming.

☐ 꽃이 떨어지나/떨어지는가(← 떨어지다) 보다.
It looks like the flower is falling.

☐ 이것이 더 크나/큰가(← 크다) 보다.
This looks bigger.

☐ 가방이 너무 무겁나/무거운가(← 무겁다) 보다.
The suitcase looks too heavy.

☐ 나는 내일 떠날까(← 떠나다) 한다.
I'm thinking of leaving tomorrow.

~아/어 있다	continuation of situation

☐ 그는 어제 한 시간 동안 이 의자에 앉아(← 앉다) 있었다.
He was sitting in this chair for an hour yesterday.

□ 장미꽃이 아름답게 활짝 피어(← 피다) 있다.
The rose is in full blossom beautifully.

~ㄹ 뻔하다	almost

□ 그는 강에 빠질(← 빠지다) 뻔했다.
He almost fell into the river.

□ 기차 출발시간에 늦을(← 늦다) 뻔했다.
It was almost late for the train departure time.

~ㄹ 법하다	reasonable, justifiable

□ 그것은 일어날(← 일어나다) 법한 사고다.
That's a reasonable accident.

□ 그 정도라면 그는 화가 날(← 나다) 법했다.
If that extent is, he was justifiably angry.

~ㄹ/~ㄴ 듯하다	as if, likely

□ 비가 올 듯하다.
It is likely to rain.

□ 그는 아직 살아 있는 듯하다.
He seems to be still alive.

4. Derived adjective (파생형용사)

1 Abstract noun(추상명사) + "~스럽다": ㅂ-불규칙형용사

The suffix of "~스럽다" adds the meaning of 'worthy', 'deserving' or 'meaningful' to 추상명사 which is 어근 of 형용사.

- 사랑스럽다: lovely, charming, pretty, sweet, cute
- 영광스럽다: glorious, honored, honorable
- 불만스럽다: unsatisfactory, discontented, displeased
- 걱정스럽다: uneasy, anxious, worrisome
- 불안스럽다/불안하다: uneasy, restless, anxious

• 죄송스럽다/죄송하다: regrettable, sorry
• 민망스럽다/민망하다: embarrassed, flustered, sorry

- [ ] 나는 사랑스러운 처녀와 결혼하고 싶다.
  I want to marry a lovely girl.

- [ ] 여러분에게 말씀드리게 되어 매우 영광스럽습니다.
  I deem it a great honor for me to address you, sirs.

Two words of each have almost similar meaning, but "~스럽다"-형용사 implies more personal feeling than "~하다"-형용사.

- [ ] 불만스러운 결과
  an unsatisfactory result

- [ ] 저의 장래가 불안스럽습니다./불안합니다.
  I feel uneasy about my future, sir.

- [ ] 죄송하지만/죄송스럽지만 같이 갈 수 없습니다.
  I regret to say that I can't go with you, sir.

2 명사+"~답다": ㅂ-불규칙형용사

The suffix of "~답다" adds the true character or real identity to all 명사 which is 어근 of 형용사 and raises the meaning of dignity, competence or qualification as 형용사.

• 사내답다/남자답다: manlike, manly, masculine
• 정치인답다: politician-like, worthy of a politician
• 나라답다: nation-like, worthy of country
• 군인답다: soldierlike, worthy of a soldier
• 어른답다: senior-like, worthy of a senior
• 신사답다: gentlemanlike, worthy of gentleman
• 숙녀답다: ladylike, worthy of lady
• 여자답다: womanly, womanlike, feminine
• 아이답다: childlike

- [ ] 나라다운(← 나라답다) 나라에서 살고 싶다.
  I want to live in a country which is worthy of country.

"군인답게" is a derived 부사 from "군인답다". →Section 18

- [ ] 그는 진정한 군인답게 매우 용감하다.
  He is very brave as worthy of a true soldier.

"~고" of "남자답고" is a connective 어미 that implies the meaning of enumeration for the following clause. And "~어야" of "여자다워야" is also a connective 어미 that implies the meaning of condition. →Section 21, 22

☐ 나는 신사답게 행동하는 사람을 좋아한다.
I like people who behave gentlemanlike.

☐ 남자는 남자답고, 여자는 여자다워야(← 여자답다) 한다.
Man should be manlike, woman should be womanlike.

☐ 그녀는 숙녀답게 행동한다.
She is ladylike in her actions.

☐ 요즘 아이들은 아이답지 않다.
These days the children are not childlike.

- "아름답다(beautiful/pretty)" is not a 파생형용사 but an original 형용사.

3 추상명사 +"~하다": 여-불규칙형용사

By adding 접미사 of "~하다" to 어근 of 추상명사 which implies the meaning of form, situation, trait or circumstance as 어근, 형용사 is derived. Some examples are as follows.

- 정직하다: honest, truthful
- 건강하다: healthy, sound
- 행복하다: happy, blessed
- 순수하다: pure, genuine
- 용감하다: brave, courageous, valiant
- 복잡하다: complicated, complex

"~면" of "말하면(← 말하다) is a connective 어미 which implies the meaning of condition or assumption. → Section 21, 22

☐ 정직하게 말하면 용서해 주겠다.
If you say honestly, I'll forgive you.

☐ 아이들은 감수성이 순수하다.
The children are pure in sensitivity.

☐ 건강한 사람은 행복하다.
Healthy people are happy.

- The following "~하다"-형용사 are not 파생형용사 but original 형용사 of which 어근 can not be used as 자립명사.
  - 시원하다: fresh, cool
  - 깨끗하다: pure, clean, chaste, innocent
  - 착하다: good, nice, good-natured, kind-hearted
  - 훌륭하다: excellent, honorable, respectable

• 까마득하다: very far away, in the long distance
• 조용하다: quiet, still, silent, calm
• 강하다: strong, powerful, hard, intense
• 약하다: weak, feeble
• 족하다: enough, sufficient
• 박하다: illiberal, stingy, strict

"~ㄹ 거야." is a colloquial expression of "~ㄹ 것이다." as 단순미래.

☐ 목욕하고 나면 시원해질 거야.
You will feel refreshed after a bath.

☐ 영수는 착한 아이다./영수는 착하다.
Yeongsu is a good child./Yeongsu is good.

☐ 그는 훌륭한 직업에 만족하고 있다.
He is satisfied with a respectable occupation.

☐ 그곳까지는 아직 까마득하다.
It is very far away yet to that place.

☐ 여자는 약하다. 그러나 어머니는 강하다.
The woman is weak. But the mother is strong.

☐ 한 달에 100만원이면 족합니다.
One million Won is enough for a month, sir.

☐ 신입사원들에게 너무 박하게 대하지 마라.
Don't be so strict to new employees.

Twinsyllabic adjective(쌍음절형용사)

쌍음절형용사 has the same characteristics as the above original "~하다"-형용사 which consists of twinsyllable as 어근 and suffix of "~하다". Some examples of 쌍음절형용사 are as follows.

• 깜깜하다: very dark, pitch-dark, throughly ignorant, unlearned
• 단단하다: hard, solid, strong, firm
• 답답하다: stifling, stuffy, anxious, oppressive, cramped
• 똑똑하다: clever, smart
• 뚱뚱하다: fat, stout, overweight, corpulent
• 시시하다: dull and flat, stupid, insignificant, trifling, worthless
• 쌀쌀하다: (weather)chilly/rather cold, (personality)cold/cold-hearted/chilly/unfriendly/unkind

• 쓸쓸하다: lonesome, solitary, desolate
• 씩씩하다: valiant, brave, gallant
• 튼튼하다: healthy, strong, solid

☐ 나는 수출과 수입에 대해서 깜깜하다.
I'm throughly ignorant about export and import.

☐ 이 목재는 쇠같이 단단하다.
This timber is as hard as iron.

"~서" is a connective 어미 which implies the meaning of reason or cause.

☐ 내 방은 작아서(← 작다) 항상 답답하게 느낀다.
Because my room is small, I feel always oppressive.

☐ 그 영화는 시시했다.
The movie was dull and flat.

"씩씩하게" and "튼튼하게" are derived 부사 from "씩씩하다" and "튼튼하다" →Section 18

☐ 어제는 말동무가 없어서 쓸쓸했다.
I felt lonesome having no friend to talk with yesterday.

☐ 한국군은 항상 씩씩하게 싸운다.
Korean soldiers are always fighting valiantly.

☐ 국방을 튼튼하게 하는 것은 대통령의 의무다.
It is the president's duty to strengthen the national defense.

4 명사 + "~롭다": ㅂ-불규칙형용사

The suffix of "~롭다" derives 명사 to 형용사 by adding the meaning of "worthy, deserving, meaningful'. "~롭다" is combined only with 추상명사 that does not have 받침자음 in the last 음절.

• 자유롭다: free, liberal
• 평화롭다: peaceful
• 슬기롭다: reasonable, wise
• 지혜롭다: wise, sagacious, understanding
• 향기롭다: aromatic, fragrant
• 호화롭다/호화스럽다: magnificent, luxurious, opulent
• 해롭다: disadvantageous, harmful
• 여유롭다: enough, sufficient, liberal, easy and graceful, comfortable

- [ ] 라일락꽃은 향기롭다.
The lilac blossom is fragrant.

- [ ] 나는 자유로운 인생을 살고 싶다.
I want to live a free life.

- [ ] 농장에 소들이 평화롭게 풀을 뜯고 있다.
The cows graze peacefully on the farm.

- [ ] 그 사람은 부자이기 때문에 여유롭게 살고 있다.
He lives comfortably because he is rich.

The following "~롭다"-형용사 are not 파생형용사 but original 형용사.

- 새롭다: new, original, novel, fresh
- 이롭다: beneficial, useful, advantageous, profitable
- 애처롭다: pitiful, pathetic, sad
- 괴롭다: painful, difficult, embarrassing
- 한가롭다/한가하다: free, idle
- 가소롭다: ridiculous, laughable, foolish
- 까다롭다: delicate and difficult, complicated

- [ ] 너의 아이디어는 매우 새롭다.
Your idea is very fresh.

- [ ] 비에 젖은 고양이가 애처롭게 울고 있었다.
The rain-soaked cat was crying plaintively.

- [ ] 목이 아파서 숨쉬기가 너무 괴롭다.
It's very difficult to breathe because my throat hurts.

- [ ] 내일은 한가롭기 때문에 공원에서 산책할 예정이다.
I'm going for a walk in the park tomorrow because I'm free.

SECTION

18 부사

Adverb

부사어(AW) as an element for the structure of sentence consists of 체언 and 부사격조사. But 부사 does not need 조사 and is redivided into 성분부사(Adverb as an element of a sentence) and 문장부사(Adverb for the whole sentence). Please, be noted that the examples of 부사 for study in this section are under the frequent usage, to say, there are still more 부사 of the same property.

1. 성분부사

성분부사 modifies 용언, other 부사 or 관형사.

1 부사 for time and date.

- 일찍: early
- 이미, 벌써: already
- 방금: just now
- 늘, 항상: always
- 오래: long, a long while
- 곧: soon
- 바로, 즉시: immediately
- 영영, 영원히: forever, permanently
- 먼저: first
- 나중에: later
- 아직: yet
- 비로서, 마침내, 드디어: at last, finally
- 가까이: almost, nearly
- 오늘: today
- 내일: tomorrow
- 모레: the day after tomowwow
- 어제: yesterday
- 그저께: the day before yesterday
- 잠시, 잠깐: a little while, a moment
- 자주, 번번이, 종종: often, many times
- 가끔, 이따금, 때때로: from time to time, sometimes
- 틈틈이, 짬짬이: at each moment of leisure, at spare moments
- 막: just, right at the moment

☐ 그는 일찍 출발했다.
He left early.

☐ 나는 방금 일어났다.
Just now I woke up.

☐ 즉시 집으로 돌아가거라.
Return home immediately.

☐ 그는 영영 떠나버렸어요.
He left forever, grandma.

- [ ] 먼저 주무십시오.
  Please, go to bed first, sir.

- [ ] 저는 아내와 가끔/이따금/때때로 산책을 합니다.
  From time to time I take a walk with my wife, sir.

- [ ] 나는 그의 질문에 바로/즉시 대답을 할 수 없었다.
  I could not answer his question immediately.

- [ ] 영수는 마침내 시험에 합격했다.
  Yeongsu finally passed the exam.

- [ ] 영희는 아직 미성년자입니다.
  Yeonghi is still a minor, sir.

- [ ] 우리는 30년 가까이 이곳에서 살았다.
  We have lived here for nearly 30 years.

- [ ] 저는 어제 한국에 도착했습니다.
  I arrived in Korea yesterday, sir.

- [ ] 영화는 지금 막 시작했다.
  The movie started just now.

2 부사 for place or location

- 멀리: far away
- 가까이: near, close
- 샅샅이: all over, in every nook and cranny
- 곳곳이: here and there, in place after place, everywhere

- [ ] 나는 집에서 멀리 걸었다.
  I walked far away from my house.

- [ ] 그는 내 집에서 가까이 살고 있다.
  He lives near from my house.

- [ ] 공원은 곳곳이 꽃으로 가득하다.
  Everywhere in the park is full of flowers.

- [ ] 그 아이는 정원을 샅샅이 뒤져서(← 뒤지다) 동전을 찾았다.
  The boy searched all over the garden and found a coin.

3 부사 for comparison

- 매우, 아주, 대단히: very, extremely
- 너무: too, too much
- 조금, 약간, 좀: slightly, somewhat, a little
- 가장, 제일: most, extremely
- 거의: almost, nearly
- 훨씬: much ~, far ~, by far
- 극히, 심히: extremely, exceedingly
- 참, 정말, 진짜: really, truly

☐ 영희는 노래를 매우/아주/대단히 잘한다.
Yeonghi sings very well.

☐ 시장은 집에서 너무 멀어요.
The market is too far from home, auntie.

☐ 희자가 우리 동네에서 제일/가장 아름다운 여학생이다.
Hija is the most beautiful female student in our village.

"더" is also 부사, meaning 'more'.

☐ 이 산이 저 산보다 약간/조금/좀 더 높다.
This mountain is slightly higher than that mountain.

☐ 악어는 사람에게 대단히/극히 위험한 동물이다.
The crocodile is an extremely dangerous animal to humans.

"다" is also 부사, meaning 'all, everybody, everything, etc'.

☐ 빵은 이제 거의 다 팔렸다.
The bread is almost sold out now.

☐ 비행기는 배보다 훨씬 빠르다.
The plane is much faster than the ship.

☐ 이 아이는 정말/참/진짜 똑똑하다.
This kid is really smart.

4 부사 for meaning "together"

- 함께, 같이: together
- 서로: each other, one another
- 모두, 다, 전부: all, all together, total

☐ 우리 함께/같이 갑시다.
Let's go together, sir.

☐ 나는 지민이와 함께/같이 차를 마셨다.
I drank tea (together) with Jimin.

☐ 그들은 서로 존경한다.
They respect each other.

☐ 모두 함께/같이 먹읍시다.
Let's all eat together, sirs.

☐ 모두/다/전부 합쳐서(← 합치다) 얼마예요?
How much is it in total, Miss ~?

☐ 우리는 그 계획에 모두/다 반대한다.
We're all against the plan.

☐ 그들은 전부/모두/다 열명이다.
They are ten in total.

5 부사 for assisting the meaning of "how to do"

- 빨리: quickly, rapidly
- 깊이: deeply
- 높이: high
- 천천히: slowly
- 잘: well, nicely
- 가만히: secretly, quietly
- 조용히: quietly, silently
- 촘촘히: closely, densely
- 대충, 대강: roughly, loosely
- 반드시, 꼭, 분명히: surely, without fail, certainly, by all means
- 스스로, 몸소: for oneself, on one's own initiative
- 저절로: of/by itself, automatically
- 다시: again, once more

☐ 이리 빨리 오세요.
Come here quickly, sir.

☐ 숨을 깊이 쉬어라.
Breathe deeply.

☐ 높이 나는 새가 멀리 본다.
The bird flying high looks far away.

☐ 여기는 좁으니까 촘촘히 앉으세요.
Please sit close together because it is narrow here, sir.

"거예요." is a colloquial 존댓말 of "것이다". And 반말 is "거다." or "거야.".

☐ 그는 반드시/꼭/분명히 올 거예요.
He will surely come, Mrs. ~.

☐ 꼭 저 차를 사고 싶습니다.
I want to buy that car by all means, sir.

☐ 그는 조용히 책을 읽었다.
He read the book quietly.

☐ 그는 일을 너무 대충 끝낸다.
He finishes working too roughly.

☐ 하늘은 스스로 돕는 자를 돕는다.
Heaven helps those who help themselves.

☐ 문이 저절로 열렸다.
The door opened by itself/automatically.

☐ 그는 편지를 다시 읽었다.
He read the letter again.

- "잘" as 부사 is used right before 동사 only very often and comfortably in conversation.

☐ 그는 노래를 잘 한다. ↔ 그는 노래를 잘 못한다.
He sings well. ↔ He can't sing well.

☐ 저는 그를 잘 압니다(←알다). ↔ 저는 그를 잘 모릅니다(←모르다).
I know him well, sir. ↔ I don't know him well, sir.

☐ 그는 피아노를 매우 잘 쳐요(←치다). ↔ 그는 피아노를 잘 못쳐요.
He plays the piano very well, Mr. ~.
↔ He can't play the piano well, Mr. ~.

☐ 잘 자(←자다). : Sleep well.(Good night.)
- Colloquial 존댓말: 안녕히 주무세요.
- High-honorific 존댓말: 안녕히 주무십시오.

☐ 잘 가(←가다).: Bye.
- Colloquial 존댓말: 안녕히 가세요.
- High-honorific 존댓말: 안녕히 가십시오.

6 부사 for echoic or mimetic expression

There are many 부사 of this type in 한국어. Here are some of them.

- 윙윙: buzzing sounds from something flying or running motor
- 멍멍, 컹컹: barking of dog, bowwow
- 흔들흔들: swayingly, rockingly
- 뭉게뭉게: rising clouds one after another, soaring smoke in great profusion
- 살살: gently, softly, lightly
- 출렁출렁: undulating of big waves
- 찰랑찰랑: lapping of ripples
- 졸졸: flowing water weakly
- 콸콸: flowing water violently
- 꼬꼬댁: cackling of chicken
- 엉금엉금: crawling or creeping such as tortoise
- 꼬불꼬불: winding or zigzag small
- 꾸불꾸불: winding or zigzag big
- 개굴개굴: croaking of frog
- 부글부글: boiling/bubbling/simmering briskly
- 보글보글: boing/bubbling/simmering weakly

☐ 꽃밭에서 벌들이 윙윙 날아다닌다.
Bees are flying around with buzz in the flower garden.

☐ 우리 개가 낯선 사람들에게 컹컹/멍멍 짖었다.
Our dogs barked(went bowwow) at strangers.

☐ 지진 때문에 건물이 흔들흔들 움직였다.
The building was shaken swayingly by the earthquake.

☐ 서쪽 하늘에 구름이 뭉게뭉게 피어올랐다.
Clouds rose up one after another in the western sky.

□ 나는 그의 어깨를 살살 마사지 해 주었다.
I gently massaged his shoulders.

□ 바다에는 파도가 출렁출렁 치고 있다.
The waves are undulating violently in the sea.

□ 비가 와서 계곡에 물이 콸콸 흐르고 있다.
The water is flowing down violently in the ravine because of rain.

□ 거북이가 엉금엉금 기어 바다로 간다.
Turtle crawls to the sea.

□ 산에 올라가는 길이 꾸불꾸불 보인다.
The path for climbing the mountain looks winding.

□ 개구리들이 논에서 개굴개굴 울고 있다.
The frogs are croaking in the rice field.

□ 작은 냄비에 라면이 보글보글 끓고 있다.
Ramen is bubbling weakly in the small pot.

7 Demonstrative adverbs

- 여기, 이리: here
- 거기, 그리: there
- 저기, 저리: there

□ 그 사람은 여기 없습니다.
He is not here, sir.

□ 그리 가세요.
Please, go there.

□ 이리 와.
Come here.

□ 저리 가.
Go away.

8 Others

- 단, 다만, 단지, 오직: only, just
- 겨우: barely, narrowly
- 별로: not particularly, not especially, not so much
- 약, 대강: approximately, about
- 특히, 특별히: especially, particularly
- 그냥: as it is, just, all the way/time, without doing anything

☐ 내 지갑에 단지/단/오직/겨우 천 원만 있다.
I have only one thousand won in my wallet.

☐ 그는 다만/오직/단지 걷기만 했다.
He was just walking.

☐ 그는 겨우 시험에 합격했다.
He had barely passed the test.

☐ 그는 특히/특별히 돼지고기를 좋아한다고 말했다.
He said he especially likes pork.

☐ 이 옷은 특별히 정국이를 위해 샀다.
This clothes was bought specially for Jeongkuk.

☐ 그는 달리기를 별로 좋아하지 않는다고 했다.
He said he doesn't like running so much.

☐ 이 돈은 약/대강 백만 원이다.
This money is about one million Won.

☐ 그 아이는 그냥 울기만 한다.
The child does nothing but cry.

2. 문장부사

문장부사 is placed usually in front of the sentence and modifies the whole sentence.

1 부사 for conclusive allusion

- 과연: indeed, as expected
- 물론: of course, undoubtedly
- 정말/정말로, 참말로, 실로: really, indeed
- 모름지기: definitely, under all circumstances, It's proper that ~
- 아무튼, 어쨌든, 하여튼: anyhow, anyway, in any case

□ 과연 그녀는 정말 아름답구나!
She is really beautiful, as expected!

□ 실로 30년 만에 그를 다시 만났다.
Indeed, after 30 years I met him again.

□ 모름지기 남자는 용감해야 한다.
It is proper that the man must be brave.

□ 물론 대한민국은 민주주의 국가입니다.
Of course, Korea is a democratic country.

□ 정말로/참말로 제주도는 아름다운 섬이다.
Indeed, Jeju Island is a beautiful island.

□ 아무튼/어쨌든/하여튼 그렇게 하겠다.
I will do so, anyway.

2 부사 for supposition

- 설마: not likely, surely not, possibly not
- 아마: maybe, perhaps
- 만일, 혹시: if, in case
- 비록, 아무리: even if, although

□ 설마 오늘 비는 안 오겠지.
It is not likely to rain today.

* "(용언)~겠지(요)." and "(체언) ~(이)겠지(요)." are the terminative 어미(종결어미) for rather strong prediction in the colloquial style.

* Colloquial 존댓말 of "~겠지요." is often abbreviated to "~겠죠.".
할머니, 오늘 비는 안 오겠지요./오겠죠(← 오다).
I don't think it will rain today, grandma.

철수는 방에서 공부하고 있겠지요./있겠죠(← 있다).
I believe that Cheolsu is studying in the room, Mr. ~.

그 아이는 초등학생이겠지(← 초등학생이다).
I guess, that boy is an elementary school student.

- [ ] 아마 그는 여기 오지 않을 것이다.
  Maybe he won't come here.

- [ ] 만일/혹시 내일 비가 오면, 경기를 연기하겠다.
  I will postpone the game if it rains tomorrow.

"~더라도" is a connective 어미(연결어미) which implies concession. → Section 21, 22

- [ ] 비록/아무리 열심히 일하더라도(←일하다/work), 돈을 벌지(←벌다/earn) 못한다.
  Even though I work hard, I can not earn money.

3 부사 for desire or request

- 제발, 부디: please
- 아무쪼록: as much as one can, to the best of one's ability

- [ ] 제발/부디 도와주십시오.
  Please, help me, sir.

- [ ] 아무쪼록 건강하시기를 바랍니다.
  I wish that you are as healthy as possible, madam.

- [ ] 제발/부디 반드시 그렇게 해 주십시오.
  Please, do so by all means, sir.

- [ ] 아무쪼록 몸조심해라.
  Take the best possible care of yourself.

4 Conjunctive adverb(접속부사) for sentence to sentence(clause to clause)

- 그리고, 또, 또한: and
- 그래서, 그러므로, 따라서: so, therefore
- 그러면: if so, then
- 그러나, 그렇지마는, 하지만: but
- 더구나: moreover, in addition
- 도리어, 오히려: on the contrary, instead
- 즉: that is, in other words, to say
- 왜냐하면: because, the reason why
- 그리고: and then

☐ 영수는 착하다. 그리고/또/또한 열심히 공부한다.
Yeongsu is kind-hearted. And he studies hard.

☐ 나는 먼저 방을 청소하고, 그리고 공부를 시작했다.
First I cleaned my room, and then started studying.

☐ 영수는 미남이다. 그래서/그러므로/따라서 나는 그를 좋아한다.
Yeongsu is handsome. So I like him.

☐ 그러면 나는 무엇을 합니까?
What do I do then, sir?

☐ 이 옷은 싸다. 그러나/그렇지마는/하지만 질기다.
This dress is cheap. But durable.

☐ 어제는 추웠다. 더구나 눈도 왔다.
It was cold yesterday. Moreover, it snowed too.

☐ 그 약을 먹고 나서 오히려/도리어 병이 나빠졌다.
After taking the medicine, the sickness got worse on the contrary.

☐ 오늘은 6월 6일, 즉 현충일이다.
Today is June 6, that is, Memorial Day.

☐ 그는 성공했다. 왜냐하면, 그는 열심히 노력했기 때문이다.
He succeeded. The reason why is that he tried hard.

5 접속부사 for word to word

- 및, 그리고, 또한: and
- 혹은, 내지, 또는: or
- 아니면: otherwise, ether ~ or, or

□ 대한민국의 영토는 한반도 및/그리고/또한 부속도서로 한다.
The territory of the Republic of Korea is the Korean Peninsula and its affiliated islands.

□ 하루 혹은/내지/또는 이틀만 기다려 주세요.
Please, wait a day or two, sir.

□ 네가 아니면 내가 잘못이다.
Either you or I am wrong.

□ 자유가 아니면 죽음을 달라(←달다).
Give me liberty, or give me death.

* "달다" means 'request something to someone' as an incomplete transitive verb(불완전타동사), and can be used for the imperative in 반말(달라. or 다오.) only.

3. Derived adverb (파생부사)

1 게-파생부사

Most of 형용사 can be converted to 부사 by using 어미 of "~게".

- 이렇다(be like this) → 이렇게(like this)
- 그렇다(be like that) → 그렇게(like that, such)
- 저렇다(be like that) → 저렇게(like that)
- 아름답다(beautiful) → 아름답게(beautifully)
- 높다(high) → 높게(highly)
- 나쁘다(bad) → 나쁘게(badly)
- 빠르다(quick) → 빠르게(quickly)
- 좋다(good) → 좋게(well)
- 강하다(strong) → 강하게(strongly)
- 시원하다(cool) → 시원하게(cooly)
- 바보스럽다(stupid) → 바보스럽게(stupidly)

□ 한글은 이렇게 씁니다.
Korean alphabet is written like this, sir.

□ 철수는 그렇게 게으른 아이가 아니다.
Cheolsu is not such a lazy kid.

□ 바람이 강하게 분다.
The wind blows strongly.

□ 그는 바보스럽게 행동한다.
He behaves stupidly.

2 이-파생부사

어미 of "~이" derives 부사 from 형용사 or 명사.

- 높다(high) → 높이(highly)
- 깨끗하다(clean) → 깨끗이(cleanly)
- 깊다(deep) → 깊이(deeply)
- 반듯하다(straight, even, orderly) → 반듯이
- 없다(There is no ~) → 없이(without)
- 나날이: day by day, every day
- 집집이: every house
- 산산이: in pieces
- 느긋하다(contented, relaxing) → 느긋이(contentedly, in relaxation)

☐ 나는 전등을 천장에 높이/높게 매달았다.
I hung the lamp high on the ceiling.

☐ 나는 방을 깨끗이/깨끗하게 청소했다.
I cleaned the room cleanly.

☐ 나는 집에서 일주일 동안 느긋이/느긋하게 쉬었다.
I took a rest in relaxation at home for a week.

☐ 그는 돈 없이 여행한다.
He travels without money.

☐ 그는 집집이 방문하였다.
He visited from house to house.

☐ 유리창이 산산이 부서졌다.
The window was smashed to pieces.

☐ 날씨는 나날이 더워졌다.
The weather got warmer day by day.

☐ 그들은 땅을 깊이/깊게 팠다.
They dug the ground deeply.

3 히-파생부사

어미 of "~히" derives 부사 from "~하다"-형용사.

- 조용하다(quiet) → 조용히/조용하게(quietly)
- 가만하다(silent, secret) → 가만히(silently, secretly)
- 천천하다(slow) → 천천히(slowly)
- 촘촘하다(close, dense) → 촘촘히/촘촘하게(closely, densely)
- 친절하다(kind) → 친절히/친절하게(kindly)

☐ 저 젊은 부부는 조용히/조용하게 얘기하고 있다.
The young couple is talking quietly.

☐ 도둑이 가만히 문을 열었다.
The thief opened the door silently.

☐ 천천히 걷자.
Let's walk slowly.

☐ 그는 밭에 포도나무를 촘촘히/촘촘하게 심었다.
He planted vines in the field densely.

☐ 그는 나를 응접실로 친절히/친절하게 안내하였다.
He kindly led me to the reception room.

SECTION

19

수동태

Passive Voice

The passive sentence(수동문) is basically the sentence of Formula 3(S+AW+P) which uses 불완전자동사(Incomplete intransitive verb) with 부사어. 불완전자동사 for 수동태 can be derived as follows.

* By the infixes(이, 히, 리, 기) as 선어말어미 in 완전타동사
* By changing 어미 of 완전타동사 with the suffix of "~아지다/~어지다"
* By changing the suffix(~하다) of "~하다-동사 which is 완전타동사 with the suffix of "~되다"

불완전자동사 which is used in 수동태 is called 피동사(Passive verb), and its antonym is 능동사(Active verb) which is used in 능동태(Active voice).

수동문 is the sentence which is transformed from Formula 4(S+O+P) by exchanging 주어 and 목적어, and by converting 완전타동사 to 불완전자동사.

* 철수가 공을 찬다(←차다/kick). → 공은 철수에 의해 차인다(←차이다).
  Cheolsu kicks ball. → Ball is kicked by Cheolsu.

부사격조사 for 부사어 in Pormula 3 are "~에", "~에게", "~에 의해" and "~한테".

* "~에게" and "~한테" are used when 체언 of AW(부사어) is the creature with heart. "~한테" is more colloquial.
* "~에" is used if 체언 of 부사어 are the creature without heart or the inanimate being.
* "~에 의해" is used for both of them in the literary style.

1. 피동사 by the infixes(이, 히, 리, 기)

"이", "히", "리" and "기" which are preceding 어미(선어말어미) can be characterized as follows, but we should keep in mind that the following characterizations always have exceptions.

1 이-피동사 from 타동사 without 받침자음 or with 받침자음(ㄱ, ㄲ, ㅎ) in the last 음절 of 어간.

- 놓이다(be put, be laid) ← 놓다(put, lay)
- 보이다(be seen) ← 보다(see)
- 묶이다(be tied) ← 묶다(tie)
- 섞이다(be mixed) ← 섞다(mix)
- 쌓이다(be piled up) ← 쌓다(pile up)
- 쓰이다(be used, be written) ← 쓰다(use, write)
- 파이다(be dug) ← 파다(dig)
- 차이다(be kicked) ← 차다(kick)

☐ 군인들에 의해 참호가 파였(← 이었)다.
Trench was dug by soldiers.

☐ 순희의 머리카락은 엄마에 의해 묶였(← 이었)다.
Sunhi's hair was tied by mother.

☐ 방에 침대가 놓였다.
A bed was laid in the room.

☐ 하늘에 비행기가 보인다.
An airplane is seen in the sky.

☐ 창고에 많은 상자가 쌓였(← 이었)다.
Many boxes were piled up in storehouse.

☐ 휘발유는 자동차 연료로 쓰인다(=사용된다).
Gasoline is used as automobile fuel.

2 히-피동사 from 타동사 with 받침자음(ㄱ, ㄺ, ㄷ, ㅂ, ㄼ, ㅈ, ㄵ) in the last 음절 of 어간.

- 닫히다(be closed) ← 닫다(close)
- 먹히다(be eaten) ← 먹다(eat)
- 박히다(be driven into) ← 박다(drive into)
- 묻히다(be buried) ← 묻다(bury)
- 씹히다(be chewed) ← 씹다(chew)
- 밟히다(be stepped on) ← 밟다(step on)
- 읽히다(be read) ← 읽다(read)
- 얹히다(be put ~ on) ← 얹다(put ~ on)
- 잡히다(be caught) ← 잡다(catch)
- 잊히다(be forgotten)←잊다(forget)

☐ 문이 바람에 닫혔(←히었)다.
The door was closed by the wind.

☐ 생선이 개에게/개한테 먹혔다.
A fish was eaten by a dog.

☐ 못이 벽에 박혔다.
A nail was driven into wall.

☐ 잔디밭이 사람들에 의해 밟히고 있다.
Lawn is being stepped on by people.

☐ 이 소설은 젊은이들에게 많이 읽힌다.
This novel is read a lot by young people.

☐ 어젯밤 도둑이 경찰에게 잡혔다.
Last night a thief was caught by the police.

☐ 남북한의 6. 25전쟁은 잊힐 수 없는 우리의 아픈 역사이다.
The Korean War between South and North Korea is our painful history that cannot be forgotten.

3 리-피동사 from 타동사 of ㄹ-불규칙동사 or ㄷ-불규칙동사, or with 받침자음(ㄹ, ㅀ) in the last 음절 of 어간.

- 뚫리다(be bored) ← 뚫다(bore)
- 들리다(be heard) ← 듣다(hear)
- 실리다(be loaded) ← 싣다(load)
- 물리다(be bitten) ← 물다(bite)
- 밀리다(be pushed) ← 밀다(push)
- 잘리다(be cut) ← 자르다(cut)
- 걸리다(be hung) ← 걸다(hang)
- 눌리다(be pressed down) ← 누르다(press down)
- 풀리다(be untied, be solved) ← 풀다(untie, solve)
- 들리다(be held, be raised) ← 들다(hold, raise)
- 깔리다(be spread, be laid) ← 깔다(spread, lay)

☐ 빵이 납작하게 눌렸(← 리었)다.
The bread was pressed down flat.

☐ 이웃집에서 노랫소리가 들린다.
Sound of song is heard from the neighbor.

☐ 쌀 포대가 부두 노무자들에 의해 배에 실렸다.
Rice bags were loaded on board by dockers.

☐ 영수는 개에게 물렸다.
Yeongsu was bitten by dog.

☐ 방바닥에 양탄자가 깔려(← 리어) 있다.
The floor of room is carpeted.

4 기-피동사 from 타동사 with 받침자음(ㄴ, ㄶ, ㄷ, ㅁ, ㅅ, ㅈ, ㅊ) in the last 음절 of 어간

- 감기다(be wound) ← 감다(wind)
- 안기다(be hugged, be embraced) ← 안다(hug, embrace)
- 찢기다(be torn) ← 찢다(tear)
- 씻기다(be washed) ← 씻다(wash)
- 뜯기다(be plucked, be torn out) ← 뜯다(pluck, tear out)
- 쫓기다(be pursued, be chased) ← 쫓다(pursue, chase)
- 끊기다(be cut off, be severed, be stopped, be turned off) ← 끊다(cut off, sever, stop, turn off)
- 담기다(be filled) ← 담다(fill)

☐ 실이 실패에 감긴다.
The thread is wound on spool.

☐ 철사 줄이 반으로 끊겼(← 기었)다.
The wire was cut in half.

☐ 아기가 엄마 품에 안겼다.
The baby was hugged in mother's arms.

☐ 신문이 찢겨(← 기어) 있다.
The newspaper has been torn.

"~서" from "씻겨서" is 연결어미 that implies the meaning of reason. →Section 21, 22

☐ 차가 빗물에 씻겨(← 기어)서 깨끗하다.
The car is clean because it was washed by rainwater.

☐ 강도들이 지금 경찰에게 쫓기고 있다.
The robbers are now being chased by the police.

2. 피동사 by the suffix of "~아지다/~어지다"

어미 of "~아지다/~어지다" converts all 타동사 into 피동사, including unconvertable 타동사 into 피동사 by the infixes(이, 히, 리, 기).

- 놓여지다/놓이다(be put, be laid) ← 놓다(put, lay)
- 닫혀지다/닫히다(be closed) ← 닫다(close)
- 뚫어지다/뚫리다(be bored) ← 뚫다(bore)
- 끊어지다/끊기다(be cut off) ← 끊다(cut off)
- 만들어지다(be made) ← 만들다(make)
- 지어지다(be built, be cooked) ← 짓다(build, cook)

☐ 자동차는 기술자들에 의해 만들어진다.
The car is made by technicians.

☐ 녹슨 철조망은 쉽게 끊어진다.
The rusted barbed-wire is easily cut.

☐ 쌀 포대가 쥐들에 의해 뜯어졌다.
The sack of rice was torn out by rats.

☐ 이 통은 계란 서른 개가 담아져 있다.
This container is filled with thirty eggs.

☐ 내 집은 목수들에 의해 지어지고 있다.
My house is being built by carpenters.

○ "~아지다/~어지다" is also used to convert 형용사 into 자동사.

- 아름답다(beautiful) → 아름다워지다(become beautiful)
- 멀다(far away) → 멀어지다(go away)
- 부지런하다(diligent) → 부지런해지다(become diligent)

3. 피동사 by the suffix of "~되다" to 어근 of "~하다"-동사

- 발견되다(be found out, be discovered) ← 발견하다(find out, discover)
- 설치되다(be installed, be set up) ← 설치하다(install, set up)
- 사용되다(be used) ← 사용하다(use)
- 평가되다(be evaluated, be appreciated) ← 평가하다(evaluate, appreciate)
- 걱정되다(be worried) ← 걱정하다(worry)
- 거듭되다(be repeated) ← 거듭하다(repeat)
- 발명되다(be invented) ← 발명하다(invent)
- 분실되다(be lost) ← 분실하다(lose)
- 수출되다(be exported) ← 수출하다(export)
- 수입되다(be imported) ← 수입하다(import)

☐ 분실된 지갑이 현관에서 발견되었다.
The lost purse was discovered at the door.

☐ 기술자에 의해 사무실에 에어컨이 설치되었다.
The air conditioner was installed in office by the mechanic.

☐ 그는 거듭된 실패 후에 마침내 성공하였다.
After repeated failures he finally succeeded.

☐ 전기는 에디슨에 의해 발명되었다.
The electricity was invented by Edison.

☐ 세종대왕의 한글자모 창제는 위대한 업적으로 평가되고 있다.
King Sejong's creation of Hangeul-alphabet is appreciated as a great achievement.

☐ 많은 자동차가 이 무역회사에 의해 수출된다.
Many cars are exported by this trading company.

☐ 할머니의 건강이 항상 걱정됩니다.
I'm always worried about my grandmother's health, madam.

SECTION

20

사동문

Causative Sentence

사동문 is made of Formula 3(S+AW+P), Formula 4(S+O+P) or Formula 5(S+AW+O+P) of the sentence structure. The causative verb(사동사) in 사동문 has the same attribute as 타동사(Transitive verb).

사동사 is derived from 용언 and can be classified as follows.

* By the infixes[이, 히, 리, 기, (이)우, 구, 추] as 선어말어미 in 용언
* By changing the suffix(~하다) of all "~하다-동사 with the suffix of "~시키다"
* 사동사 of "~시키다" can be transformed to "~을/~를 시키다".
* 보조동사(~게 하다) can convert all 용언 for 사동문

사동문 of Formula 5(S+AW+O+P) is called as the ordinary 사동문 which can be compared to the English sentence which uses 사동사 such as "have, let, make, get, help".

부사격조사 for AW in Formula 3 and Formula 5 are "~에", "~에게", "~(으)로 하여금" and "~한테" and the usage is the same as 부사격조사 for 수동태. "~(으)로 하여금" has the same attribute as "~에 의해". → Section 19
And be noted that 사동사 in Fomula 4 does not need these above 부사격조사 due to the attribute of 완전타동사.

1. 사동사 by the infixes [이, 히, 리, 기, (이)우, 구, 추]

Some 사동사 with the infixes(이, 히, 리, 기) have the same form as 피동사 like "읽히다(be read, have ~ read)". And be noted that there are exceptions in usage of these infixes like 피동사.

1 이-사동사

- 끓이다(boil, make ~ boiling) ← 끓다(boil)
- 녹이다(melt, dissolve) ← 녹다(melt)
- 속이다(cheat, deceive) ← 속다(be cheated/deceived)
- 죽이다(kill) ← 죽다(die)
- 줄이다(reduce, decrease) ← 줄다(be reduced/decreased, get smaller)
- 누이다(make ~ defecate/urinate) ← 누다(defecate, urinate)
- 먹이다(let ~ eat, feed) ← 먹다(eat)
- 높이다(heighten, raise) ← 높다(high)

☐ 나는 주전자로 물을 끓였(← 이었)다./끓게 하였다.
I boiled the water with a kettle.

☐ 따뜻한 햇볕이 얼음을 녹인다./녹게 한다.
Warm sunshine melts ice.

☐ 그는 친구를 속였다./속게 하였다.
He deceived the friend.

☐ 나는 파리채로 파리를 죽였다./죽게 하였다.
I killed a fly with a flapper

☐ 엄마는 아기에게 똥을 누였다./누게 하였다.
Mother made her baby defecate.

☐ 종석이는 염소에게 풀을 먹였다./먹게 하였다.
Jongseok fed the goat grass.

☐ 그는 조국의 명예를 높였다./높게 하였다.
He raised the honor of his fatherland.

2 히-사동사

- 눕히다(lay, make ~ lie down) ← 눕다(lie)
- 맞히다(hit, strike) ← 맞다(be hit/struck)
- 앉히다(seat, have ~ sit down) ← 앉다(sit down, take a seat)
- 익히다(cook, make ripe) ← 익다(get cooked, ripen, get well-done)
- 잡히다(let ~ mortgaged) ← 잡다(mortgage)
- 입히다(dress, clothe) ← 입다(put on, wear, be dressed, clothe oneself)
- 읽히다(have ~ read) ← 읽다(read)
- 식히다(cool, chill, let ~ cool) ← 식다(get cold, become cool)
- 좁히다(make narrow) ← 좁다(narrow)
- 넓히다(widen, broaden, enlarge) ← 넓다(wide, broad, spacious)
- 밝히다(brighten, make clear) ← 밝다(bright)

☐ 간호사는 환자를 침대에 눕혔(← 히었)다./눕게 하였다.
The nurse laid the patient in bed.

☐ 그는 총으로 과녁을 맞혔다./맞게 하였다.
He hit the target with a gun.

☐ 엄마는 망고를 상자 속에서 익히는 중이다./익게 하는 중이다.
Mom is ripening mango inside the box.

☐ 나는 돈을 빌리기 위해 은행에 집을 잡혔다./잡게 하였다.
I let my house mortgaged by the bank to borrow money.

☐ 나는 아들에게 책을 읽혔다./읽게 하였다.
I let my son read a book.

☐ 시장은 건설회사로 하여금 시청의 입구를 넓혔다./넓게 하였다.
The mayor let the construction company widen the entrance of the city hall.

3 리-사동사

- 날리다(fly, let ~ fly) ← 날다(fly)
- 돌리다(turn, rotate, spin) ← 돌다(turn round, rotate, spin)
- 살리다(keep ~ alive, let ~ live, save a person's life) ← 살다(live)
- 알리다(let ~ know, inform ~ of) ← 알다(know, have knowledge of)
- 울리다(make ~ cry/weep) ← 울다(cry, weep)
- 들리다(have ~ hold, let ~ raise) ← 들다(hold/take in one's hand)
- 얼리다(freeze, turn ~ into ice) ← 얼다(freeze, be frozen)
- 걸리다(let ~ walk) ← 걷다(walk)

☐ 영수는 지금 바닷가에서 연을 날리고 있다./날게 하고 있다.
Yeongsu flies a kite on the beach.

☐ 현복이는 팽이를 돌립니다./돌게 하고 있습니다.
Hyeonbok spins a top, sir.

☐ 신은 죽은 사람을 살릴 수 있다./살게 할 수 있다.
God can save the life of the dead.

☐ 자웅이는 시험합격을 부모님에게 알렸(← 리었)다./알게 하였다.
Jaung informed the success of the test to parents.

☐ 너는 왜 아이를 울리느냐?/울게 하느냐?
Why are you making the child cry?

☐ 나는 아기의 손에 장난감을 들렸다./들게 하였다.
I have the baby hold a toy in hand.

☐ 냉장고를 이용해서 물을 얼렸다./얼게 하였다.
I froze water by the refrigerator.

☐ 아기를 걸리지 마라./걷게 하지마라.
Do not let the baby walk.

4 기-사동사

- 남기다(leave behind, bequeath, make a profit, leave undone) ← 남다(be left over, remain)
- 숨기다(hide, conceal, put out of sight, keep secret) ← 숨다(hide/conceal oneself, be in hiding)
- 웃기다(make ~ laugh) ← 웃다(laugh)
- 옮기다(infect) ← 옮다(be infected)
- 안기다(let/have ~ hold in the arms) ← 안다(hold in one's arms, hug, embrace)
- 뜯기다(put ~ to graze) ← 뜯다(graze)
- 벗기다(strip/divest ~ of) ← 벗다(take off, strip oneself)
- 맡기다(entrust ~ with, put in a person's custody) ← 맡다(keep in trust, take charge of)
- 신기다(have ~ put on footwear) ← 신다(put on footwear)

☐ 음식을 남기지 마라.
Don't leave food.

☐ 나는 돈을 양말 속에 숨겼(← 기었)다.
I hid the money in my socks.

☐ 그의 농담은 많은 사람을 웃겼다./웃게 하였다.
His jokes made many people laugh.

☐ 그는 나에게 감기를 옮겼다.
He infected me with his cold.

☐ 나는 강아지를 영순이에게 안겼다.
I had Yeongsun hold the puppy in her arms.

☐ 나는 소들에게 풀밭에서 풀을 뜯겼다.
I put cows to graze in the grass.

☐ 엄마는 아이한테서 젖은 옷을 벗겼다.
The mother stripped the child of his wet clothes.

☐ 나는 강아지를 이웃집에 맡겼다.
I entrusted my neighbor with my puppy.

☐ 간호사는 환자에게 신발을 신겼다.
The nurse got the patient to put on shoes.

5 (이)우-사동사

- 깨우다(wake ~up from sleep) ← 깨다(wake up)
- 비우다(empty, clear out, evacuate) ← 비다(empty, vacant, unoccupied)
- 새우다(stay up all night, keep awake all night) ← (밤, 날)새다(dawn, break)
- 피우다(bloom, blossom, kindle, make a fire) ← (꽃, 불)피다(bloom, flower, burn, be kindled)
- 찌우다(fatten) ← (살)찌다(grow fat, gain weight)
- 지우다(make ~ carry on one's back, burden, put a load on ~) ← 지다(carry on the back, bear)
- 세우다(make stand, erect, stop, bring to a stop) ← 서다(stand up, stop)
- 재우다(put ~ to sleep) ← 자다(sleep)
- 채우다(fill, make full) ← 차다(fill, become full)
- 태우다(burn, put into the fire, take ~ on board, let ~ ride, give a ride) ← 타다(burn, blaze, glow, ride, take a ride, get on, go aboard)
- 돋우다(raise, make higher) ← 돋다(come up, rise)

☐ 내일 새벽에 너를 깨우겠다.
I will wake you up early morning tomorrow.

☐ 쓰레기통을 비워라.
Empty the trash can.

☐ 나는 친구 아버지의 장례식장에서 밤을 새웠(← 우었)다.
I stayed up all night at my friend's father's funeral.

☐ 따뜻한 날씨는 일찍 꽃을 피운다./피게 한다.
The warm climate bloomes the flowers early.

☐ 그는 살을 찌우기 위해 많이 먹는다.
He eats a lot to gain weight.

☐ 나는 그에게 짐을 조금만 지웠다./지게 하였다.
I put a little load on him.

☐ 누가 쓰레기를 태웠느냐?/타게 하였느냐?
Who burned the trash?

☐ 나는 쌀로 단지를 채웠다./차게 하였다.
I filled the pot with rice.

☐ 나는 집을 짓기 위해 땅을 돋우었다./돋게 하였다.
I raised the ground to build a house.

6 구-사동사

• 달구다(heat, make hot) ← 달다(become hot)

☐ 대장장이는 쇠를 숯불로 뜨겁게 달구었다.
The blacksmith heated the iron hot over charcoal fire.

7 추-사동사

• 낮추다(lower, bring down, make low) ← 낮다(low)
• 늦추다(slow down, make slow, postpone, delay) ← 늦다(late, slow)
• 맞추다(set, fit into, put together) ← 맞다(be right/correct, agree, suit, strike on)
• 들추다(raise, disclose, reveal) ← 들다(hold, have in hand, mention, state)

☐ 그는 사과의 가격을 낮추었다.
He lowered the price of apple.

☐ 우리는 회의를 세 시간 늦추었다.
We delayed the meeting three hours.

☐ 나는 자명종을 정각 여섯 시에 맞추었다.
I set the alarm clock at six o'clock.

☐ 그는 나의 비밀을 사람들에게 들추었다.
He revealed my secret to the people.

8 Abnormal 사동사

• 없애다(get rid of, clear, eliminate) ← 없다(not existing, absent)
• 적시다(get/have ~ wet) ← 젖다(get wet, be wet)
• 일으키다(make stand, raise, arouse) ← 일다(rise, get up, happen)
• 돌이키다(reflect on, look back, let go back) ← 돌다(turn round, spin, go round)

☐ 그는 집에서 위험한 물건을 전부 없앴다.
He eliminated all dangerous things at home.

☐ 그는 걸레를 물에 적시었다.
He got the rag wet with water.

☐ 유능한 대통령은 나라의 경제를 일으킨다.
An able president raises the country's economy.

☐ 불쾌한 추억은 돌이키지 마라.
Don't look back on unpleasant memories.

2. 사동사 by the suffix of "~시키다" to all "~하다"-동사

- 일시키다(have ~ work/serve) ← 일하다(work, labor)
- 공부시키다(let ~ study/learn) ← 공부하다(study, learn)
- 정지시키다(stop, make an end to ~) ← 정지하다(stop, halt)
- 식사시키다(feed, let ~ eat, let ~ have a meal) ← 식사하다(eat, have a meal)

☐ 장애인들에게 일시키지 마세요.
Please, don't have the handicapped persons work.

☐ 자녀들에게 공부시키는 것은 부모의 의무다.
It is the duty of parents to let their children study.

☐ 경찰은 빨간 차를 정지시켰다.
The police stopped the red car.

☐ 우리 학교는 11시부터 학생들을 식사시킨다.
Our school feeds students from 11 o'clock.

3. 사동문 by 타동사 of "(~을/~를) 시키다" to all "~하다"-동사

- 일을 시키다 ← 일하다
- 공부를 시키다 ← 공부하다
- 식사를 시키다 ← 식사하다
- 등산을 시키다(have ~ climb a mountain) ← 등산하다(climb a mountain)
- 여행을 시키다(have ~ travel/tour) ← 여행하다(make a trip, tour, travel)

☐ 장애인들에게 일을 시키지 마세요.

☐ 자녀들에게 공부를 시키는 것은 부모의 의무다.

☐ 우리 학교는 11시부터 학생들에게 식사를 시킨다.

☐ 나는 아이들한테 자주 등산을 시킨다.
I have my children climb the mountain often.

☐ 아이들에게 일 년에 한 번씩 해외여행을 시킨다.
I have my children travel abroad once a year.

4. 사동문 by 보조동사(~게 하다) to all 용언

- 놀게 하다(let ~ play) ← 놀다(play)
- 가게 하다(have ~ go) ← 가다(go)
- 먹게 하다(have ~ eat) ← 먹다(eat)
- 사게 하다(let ~ buy) ← 사다(buy)
- 공부하게 하다(have ~ study) ← 공부하다(study)
- 밝게 하다(make ~ bright) ← 밝다(bright)
- 편리하게 하다(make ~ convenient) ← 편리하다(convenient)
- 타게 하다(let ~ ride) ← 타다(ride)
- 웃게 하다(have ~ laugh) ← 웃다(laugh)
- 마시게 하다(have ~ drink) ← 마시다(drink)
- 어렵게 하다(make ~ difficult) ← 어렵다(difficult)
- 있게 하다 (let ~ be/exist/stay) ← 있다(be, exist, stay)

☐ 나는 아이들을 정원에서 놀게 했다.
I let my children play in the garden.

☐ 나는 아들을 일찍 학교에 가게 했다.
I have my son go to school early.

☐ 엄마는 딸에게 약을 먹게 했다.
The mother had her daughter take medicine.

☐ 선생님은 영수에게 수학을 더 열심히 공부하게 했다.
The teacher made Yeongsu study mathematics harder.

☐ 어머니는 제가 먹고 싶은 과일을 사게 했습니다.
My mother let me buy the fruit that I wanted to eat, sir.

☐ 그는 할머니의 방을 더 밝게 했다.
He made the grandmother's room brighter.

☐ 발명가는 인간의 삶을 편리하게 합니다.
The inventor makes human life convenient, sir.

☐ 그는 나를 그의 차에 타게 했다.
He let me ride on his car.

☐ 능력 없는 사장은 회사를 어렵게 한다.
An incompetent boss makes a company hard.

☐ 그의 농담은 많은 사람을 웃게 했다.
His jokes made many people laugh.

5.

Negative 사동문 (부정사동문)

"(용언)~지 않게 하다" and "(용언)~지 못하게 하다" are used for 부정사동문. → Section 10

☐ A: 나는 아이들을 정원에서 놀지 않게 했다.
I didn't let the kids play in the garden.

B: 나는 아이들을 정원에서 놀지 못하게 했다.
I kept the kids from playing in the garden.

☐ A: 나는 아들을 너무 일찍 학교에 가지 않게 한다.
I have my son not go to school too early.

B: 나는 아들을 너무 일찍 학교에 가지 못하게 한다.
I keep my son from going to school too early.

☐ A: 엄마는 딸에게 그 약을 먹지 않게 했다.
The mother had her daughter not take the medicine.

B: 엄마는 딸에게 그 약을 먹지 못하게 했다.
The mother kept her daughter from taking the medicine.

SECTION

21

용언의 어미변화 I

Inflection of 어미 for 용언 I

한국어 has many types of 어미변화 for 용언, including 서술격조사. These types of inflection provide several functions which are mood, tense, honorific, modesty, conjugation and conjunction. This means that 어미변화 is the most complicate part in 한국어. It is said that the types of 어미변화 for 용언 and 서술격조사 are counted about 1,760 in all.

1. Structure of 어미

The practical 어미 consists of the final 어미(어말어미) for type(mood) of sentence and conjunction, and the preceding 어미(선어말어미) for honorific, modesty and tense. Therefore the infinitive of 용언 has no 선어말어미.

어말어미 is redivided into the terminative 어미(종결어미) about 20% and the connective 어미(연결어미) about 80% for the compound and complex sentence.

Examples of 어미

1 쓰다: write

선생님께서 칠판에 "조용히!"라고 쓰셨(← 시었)습니다.
The teacher wrote "Be quiet." on the board, sir.

- 쓰: 어간
- 시: 선어말어미 for 높임표현 to the 3. person
- 었: 선어말아미 for 과거시제
- 습니: 선어말어미 for the literary 높임표현 to the person spoken
- 다: 종결어미

2 먹다: eat

저는 나중에 혼자 먹겠습니다.
I'll eat alone later, sir.

- 먹: 어간
- 겠: 선어말어미 for 의지미래 of the person speaking
- 습니: 선어말어미 for the literary 높임표현 to the person spoken
- 다: 종결어미

3 공부하다(여-불규칙동사): study

너는 어제 정말 열심히 공부했(←하였)구나!
You studied really hard yesterday!

- 공부하: 어간
- 였: 선어말어미 for 과거시제
- 구나: 종결어미 for exclamation in 반말 to the person spoken

4 **배우다: learn, 재미있다: funny, interesting**

아빠, 저는 영어를 배우니까 재미있어요.
I have fun because I learn English, daddy.

- 배우: 어간
- 니까: 연결어미 for the meaning of reason
- 재미있: 어간
- 어요: 종결어미 for the colloquial 높임표현 to the person spoken.

2. List of typical 연결어미

Application	연결어미
enumeration (나열)	~고, ~(으)며
simultaneity (동시성)	~(으)면서, ~자, ~자마자
sequence/order (순서)	~고, ~(아/어)서
change of circumstance/action (상황/행위의 전환)	~다가, ~다
opposition(대립), contrast(대조)	~(으)나, ~지만, ~ㄴ데/~는데/~은데, ~(아/어)도
reason(이유), cause(원인)	~(아)서/(어)서, ~(으)니까, ~(으)므로, ~느라고
condition(조건), assumption(가정)	~(으)면, ~(으)려면, ~(이)라면, ~(아/어)야
purpose(목적), intention(의도)	~(으)러, ~(으)려고, ~게
concession (양보)	~(아/어)도, ~ㄹ지라도/ ~을지라도, ~더라도
selection (선택)	~거나, ~든, ~든지, ~든가
method(방법), means(수단)	~(아/어)서, ~고
background (배경)	~ㄴ데/~는데/~은데, ~(으)니

3. Distinctive features of 연결어미 and example sentences

1 Enumeration: ~고, ~(으)며

1. Both connect the clauses coordinately without other meaning.
2. To emphasize the meaning of coordinate enumeration, 접속부사 of "그리고(and, as well as) can be added.
3. For 과거시제, "~고" has no problem even though 선어말어미(~았/었~) is not used, but "~(으)며 should use "~았/었~".
4. For 미래시제 of both, 선어말어미(~겠~) can be be omitted.
5. "~(으)며" does not match with 청유문 and 명령문.

- [ ] 비가 오고/오며 (그리고) 바람이 분다.
  It's raining and windy.
- [ ] 어제는 비가 오고/왔고/왔으며 (그리고) 바람도 불었다.
  It was raining yesterday and windy too.
- [ ] 내일은 비가 오고/오겠고/오며/오겠으며 바람도 불 것이다.
  It will rain and windy too tomorrow.
- [ ] 영수는 키가 크고/크며 (그리고) 미남이다.
  Yeongsu is tall and handsome.
- [ ] 영수는 키가 크고/크며 갑제는 키가 작다.
  Yeongsu is tall and Gapje is short.
- [ ] 승기는 공부도 못하고/못하며 운동도 못한다.
  Seunggi is not good at studying nor at sports.
- [ ] 바나나도 먹고 망고도 먹어라.
  Eat bananas and mangoes too.
- [ ] 나는 고등학생이고/고등학생이며 형은 대학생이다.
  I'm a highschool student, ang my elder brother is a university student.
- [ ] 강은 맑고/맑으며 하늘은 푸르다.
  The river is clear and the sky is blue.

2 Simultaneity of occurrences: ~(으)면서, ~자, ~자마자

1. If necessary to emphasize simultaneity specially, 부사어 of "동시에(at the same time)" can be added.
2. 선어말어미(~았/었~, ~겠~) for tense can not be used.
3. All of these do not match with 부정문.
4. "~으면서" is used when the last 음절 of 어간 has 받침자음.
5. When "~으면서" and "~자" are combined to 형용사 or 서술격조사, the meaning of enumeration is added.
6. "~자" matches with 동사 and 서술격조사, but "~자마자" match with 동사 only.
7. "~자" doesn't match with 명령문, 청유문 and 의문문.

- ▢ 우리는 등산을 하면서 이야기를 했다.
  We talked while climbing mountain.
- ▢ 나는 피아노를 치면서 노래를 불렀다.
  I sang while playing the piano.
- ▢ 열이 나면서 (동시에) 머리도 아프다.
  I have a fever and a headache (at the same time).
- ▢ 그는 학생이면서/학생이자 영화배우다.
  He is a student and a movie star.
- ▢ 커피 마시면서 쉬어라.
  Take a break with a cup of coffee.
- ▢ 이 신발은 싸면서 질기다.
  These shoes are cheap and durable.
- ▢ 우리는 과일을 먹으면서 텔레비전을 보았다.
  We watched TV while eating fruit.
- ▢ 집을 나서자/나서자마자 (동시 에) 비가 오기 시작했다.
  No sooner had I left home than it began to rain.
- ▢ 까마귀 날자 배 떨어진다.
  Right after a crow flies from the tree, a pear falls.

☐ 그녀는 나를 만나자마자 울기 시작했다.
On seeing me, she began crying.

☐ 어이구, 너는 영화가 시작하자마자 (동시에) 자는구나!
Oh my, you fall asleep right after the start of movie!

3 Sequence of occurrences: ~고, ~(아/어)서

1. 주어 of each clause should be same.
2. 선어말어미 for tense can not be used.
3. Both match with **동사** only and don't match with **부정문**.
4. When the condition of the first clause has an effect on the following clause, "~(아/어)서" is used, but otherwise "~고" or is used.
5. "**~고 나서**" from **보조동사** of "**~고 나다**" is more definite than "~고" for the meaning of sequence of occurrences.
6. In case of "**~고**" or "**~고 나서**", **접속부사** of "**그리고**(and then)" can be added to emphasize the meaning of sequence of occurences.

☐ 그는 옷을 벗고/벗고 나서 (그리고) 침대에 누웠다.
He took off clothes and (then) lay on the bed.

☐ 나는 아침을 먹고/먹고 나서 (그리고) 학교에 갔다.
After breakfast I went to school.

☐ 나는 방을 청소하고 (그리고) 아침식사를 했다.
I cleaned the room and I had breakfast.

☐ 옷을 벗어서 옷장에 넣었다.
I took off clothes and put them in the closet.

☐ 나는 과일을 씻어서 먹었다.
I washed the fruit and ate it.

☐ 운전면허증을 지갑에 넣어서 책상 위에 두었다.
I put my driver's license in walet and put it on the desk.

4 Change of circumstance or action: ~다가, ~다

1. Both do not match with 미래시제. For 과거시제, "~았/었~" can be used to "~다가" , but not possible to "~다".

2. If the circumstance or action of the preceding and following clauses are same, 주어 of clauses can be different, but if not same, 주어 of each clause should be same.

3. "~다가" is used more often than "~다".

- ▢ 그는 아침을 먹다가/먹다 전화를 받았다.
  While eating breakfast, he received a call.
- ▢ 그는 회사에 출근하다가/출근하다 집으로 돌아왔다.
  While going to the company, he returned home.
- ▢ 그는 회사에 출근했다가 집으로 돌아올 것이다.
  He will return home after he enters the company.
- ▢ 오전에는 내가 가축들을 돌보다가 오후에는 형이 가축들을 돌본다.
  In the morning I take care of the cows, and in the afternoon my brother takes care of them.
- ▢ 집 바깥이 조용하다가 갑자기 시끄럽다.
  The outside of house was quiet, but suddenly noisy.
- ▢ 그는 선생이었다가 이제는 사업가이다.
  He was a teacher and now is a businessman.
- ▢ 여기서 잠깐 쉬다가 가자.
  Let's rest here for a moment and then go.

5 Opposition//Contrast: ~(으)나, ~지만, ~ㄴ데/~는데/~은데, ~(아/어)도

1. When the contents of preceding and following clause are contrary or different, these 연결어미 are used.
2. All except "~(아/어)도" should use 선어말어미 for tense.
3. "~(아/어)도" uses "~았/었~" for 과거시제, but doesn't use "~겠~" for 미래시제.
4. "~(으)나" and "~ㄴ데/~는데/~은데" do not match well with 청유문 and 명령문.

☐ 영수는 키가 크지만/크나/큰데/커도 칠성이는 키가 작다.
Yeongsu is tall but Chilseong is short.

☐ 설탕은 물에 녹으나/녹지만/녹는데/녹아도 식용유는 녹지 않는다.
The sugar dissolves in water but not the cooking oil.

☐ 나는 그녀를 사랑했으나/사랑했지만/사랑했는데/사랑했어도 그녀는 나를 사랑하지 않았다.
I loved her but she didn't love me.

☐ 너는 성인이나/성인이지만/성인인데/성인이어도 미성년자보다 못하다.
You are an adult but you are inferior to a minor.

☐ 그는 영어는 못 하나/하지만/하는데/해도 일본어는 잘 한다.
He can not speak English but speaks Japanese well.

SECTION

22

용언의 어미변화 II

Inflection of 어미 for 용언 II

Korean Proverb(한국 속담)

가는 말이 고와야 오는 말이 곱다.
Nice words for nice words.
If the word you say is good, then the word coming back is good.

고기는 씹어야 맛이고 말은 해야 맛이다.
Meat tastes by chewing, and word tastes by saying.
Feelings are meant to be expressed.

낮말은 새가 듣고 밤말은 쥐가 듣는다.
Walls have ears.
Refrain from speaking ill of other people.
Daytimes birds listen, and nighttimes mice listen.

발 없는 말이 천리를 간다.
Words run thousands of miles even without feet.
Bad news has wings.

1. Reason/Cause: ~(아/어)서, ~(으)니까, ~(으)므로, ~느라고

1. All connect the clauses when the preceding clause contains reason or cause for the following clause.
2. "~(으)니까" and "~(으)므로" can omit "~았/었~" for 과거시제, but can not omit "~겠~" for 미래시재.
3. "~(아/어)서" and "~느라고" do not use any 선어말어미 for tense.
4. When "~느라고" is used, 주어 of each clause should be same and be the creature with heart.
5. "~느라고" matches with 동사 only and can not be combined to negative clause.
6. "~(아/어)서", "~(으)므로" and "~느라고" do not match with 청유문 and 명령문.
7. In case of "~느라고", the content of following clause is contrary or negative to the reason or cause of the preceding clause.

- ▢ 방이 넓어서/넓으니까/넓으므로 아이들이 좋아한다.
  The children are happy because the room is spacious.

- ▢ 영수는 발이 아파서/아프니/아프니까/아프므로 더 걸을 수 없다.
  Yeongsu can not walk more because his foot is sore.

- ▢ 택시를 타서/타니까(탔으니까)/타므로(탔으므로) 늦지 않았다.
  I was not late bacause I took taxi.

- ▢ 아이들을 잘 돌보겠으니까/돌보겠으므로 걱정하지 마세요.
  Don't worry because I will take good care of the children, Mrs. ~.

- ▢ 숙제를 하느라고 잠을 못 잤다.
  I didn't sleep because of doing homework.

- ▢ 어제는 친구들과 노느라고(←놀다) 숙제를 못 했다.
  Didn't do homework because I played with friends yesterday.

- ▢ 늦었으니까/늦었으므로 택시를 타자.
  Let's take a taxi because we are late.

☐ 나는 수영을 못해서/못하니까/못하므로 바다에 안 간다.
I don't go to the sea because I can not swim.

- "때문에" which is 부사어 and used very often as a conjunctive word has also the meaning of reason or cause. →Section 14, 의존명사

1 명사 + "~ 때문에"

☐ 너 때문에 학교에 늦었다.
I was late to school because of you.

☐ 돈 때문에 은행에 갔다.
Because of money I went to the bank.

2 동명사 or 형용명사: "~ㅁ/~음/~움 때문에"

☐ 너의 아름다움 때문에 너를 좋아한다.
Because of your beauty I like you.

☐ 아버지의 죽음 때문에 슬프다.
I'm sad because of father's death.

3 동명사 or 형용명사: "~기 때문에", "~ㅆ기 때문에(과거시제)"

☐ 택시를 타기 때문에 늦지 않는다.
I will not be late because I take a taxi.

☐ 물을 마셨기 때문에 목이 마르지 않다.
I'm not thirsty because I drank water.

☐ 예쁘기 때문에 너를 좋아한다.
I like you because you are pretty.

4 서술격조사: "~기 때문에"

☐ 그는 택시를 탈 예정이기 때문에 늦지 않을 것이다.
He will not be late because he will take a taxi.

☐ 그는 회사의 사장이기 때문에 바쁘다.
He is busy because he is a boss of a company.

☐ 저것은 목재이기 때문에 물에 뜬다(←뜨다).
Because that is wood, that floats on water.

2. Condition/Assumption: ~(으)면, ~(이)면, ~(이)라면, ~(아/어)야

1 All connect the clauses when the content of following clause is under the condition or assumption of the preceding clause.

2 "~(이)면" at "~(이)라면" match with **서술격조사** only.

3 All except "~(이)라면" use "~았/었~" for **과거시제**.

4 All do not use "~겠~" for **미래시제**.

5 "~(으)면" with "~겠~" expresses the guess for **현재시제** of the person speaking.

- ☐ 모르겠으면 질문해라.
  If you don't understand, ask me questions.
- ☐ 네가 못 하겠으면 내가 하겠다.
  If you can not do, I will do.
- ☐ 떠나겠으면 미리 준비하세요.
  If you are going to leave, prepare in advance, please.

6 "~(아)야/(어)야" implies the meaning of condition and does not match with **청유문** and **명령문**.

☐ 노래를 잘 Ⓐ부르면/Ⓑ불러야 상을 탈 수 있다.
Ⓐ If you sing well, you can win a prize.
Ⓑ Based on good singing, you can win a prize.

☐ 너는 어제 노래를 잘 Ⓐ불렀으면/Ⓑ불렀어야 상을 탈 수 있었다.
Ⓐ If you sang well yesterday, you could win a prize.
Ⓑ You should have sung well yesterday in order to win a prize.

☐ 시험성적이 Ⓐ좋으면/Ⓑ좋아야 합격할 것이다.
Ⓐ If you have good test score, you will pass.
Ⓑ Under the condition that the test score is good, you will pass.

☐ 부지런한 Ⓐ사람이면/Ⓑ사람이어야 부자가 될 수 있다.
Ⓐ If you are diligent, you can become rich.
Ⓑ Only diligent people can become rich.

- ☐ 내가 Ⓐ너라면/Ⓑ학생이라면 공부만 열심히 하겠다.
  Ⓐ If I were you, I would only study hard.
  Ⓑ If I were a student, I would only study hard.

- ☐ 아빠가 도착하면 함께 식사하자.
  When daddy arrives, let's eat together.

- ☐ 네가 안 가면 내가 가겠다.
  If you don't go, I'll go.

- ☐ 고기를 적게 먹어야 날씬해진다.
  You should eat less meat to slim down.

- "~라면" is also used as an abbreviated 연결어미 of "~라고 하면" which means 'as you are told ~', 'as I tell you ~' or 'if you say ~'.

  - ☐ 가라면(가라고 하면) 가.
    Go as you are told.
  - ☐ 먹으라면(먹으라고 하면) 먹어야 한다.
    You should eat as I tell you.
  - ☐ 유기농 채소라면(채소라고 하면) 사겠다.
    If you say that it is organic vegetable, I'll buy.
  - ☐ 그 사람이 영철이라면(영철이라고 하면) 만나겠다.
    If you say that he is Yeongcheol, I'll meet him.

3. Purpose/Intention: ~(으)러, ~(으)려고, ~게

1. All connect the clauses when the content of the preceding clause is purpose or intention and the following clause is for fulfillment of the purpose or intention.
2. All match with 동사 only and do not use 선어말어미 for tense.
3. Except "~게", 주어 of each clause should be same, and should be human or animal.

4 "~(으)려고" doesn't match with 청유문 and 명령문.

5 "~(으)러" doesn't match with 부정문.

- ☐ 축구하러/축구하려고 운동장에 간다.
  We go to the playground to play soccer.

- ☐ 살을 빼려고 굶는 중이다.
  I'm starving to lose weight.

- ☐ 저는 시험을 잘 보려고 공부하고 있어요.
  I am studying to take the test well, Mama.

"~려고 하면" can be abbreviated to "~려면".

- ☐ 늦지 않으려고(←않다) 하면/않으려면 서둘러라.
  Hurry up if you don't want to be late.

- ☐ 빨리 도착하려고 하면/도착하려면 비행기로 가거라.
  If you want to arrive quickly, go by plane.

- ☐ 아버지가 주무시게 이불을 펴 드렸다.
  I laid out a quilt for dad to sleep on.

- ☐ 정원이 보이게 영수는 창문을 열었다.
  Yeongsu opened the window so that the garden could be seen.

- ☐ 영화를 보러 극장에 가자.
  Let's go to the theater to see a movie.

- ☐ 아기가 잠들 수 있게 조용히 해라.
  Be quiet for the baby to fall asleep.

"(동명사)~기 위해/위하여" is a conjunctive word also for purpose or intention. "위해" is 준말 of "위하여".

- 축구하기 위해 운동장에 간다.
- 살을 빼기 위해 굶는 중이다.
- 저는 시험을 잘 보기 위하여 공부하고 있어요.

4. Concession: ~(아/어)도, ~(ㄹ/을)지라도, ~더라도

1. All connect the clauses when the content of the following clause is contrary to the preceding clause under concession.
2. All use "~았/었~" for 과거시제, but do not use "~겠~" for 미래시제.
3. 부사 of "비록" or "아무리" can be used together to emphasize the meaning of concession.

- ☐ (비록) 시험에 떨어져도/떨어질지라도/떨어지더라도 실망하지 않겠다.
  I will not be disappointed even if I fail in the test.
- ☐ 그는 시험에 떨어졌어도/떨어졌을지라도/떨어졌더라도 실망하지 않았다.
  He was not disappointed even though he failed in the test.
- ☐ 아무리 힘들어도/힘들지라도/힘들더라도 그는 포기하지 않는다.
  No matter how hard it is, he doesn't give up.
- ☐ 아무리 날씨가 나빠도/나쁠지라도/나쁘더라도 우리는 내일 등산하겠다.
  No matter how bad the weather is, we will climb mountain tomorrow.
- ☐ 그 일은 누가 해도/하더라도/할지라도 결과는 같을 것이다.
  No matter who does that work, the result will be same.
- ☐ 이 일은 누가 했어도/했더라도/했을지라도 결과는 같다.
  No matter who did this work, the result is the same.
- ☐ 네가 아무리 가난해도/가난하더라도/가난할지라도 누가 너를 도울까?
  No matter how poor you are, who will help you?
- ☐ 네가 비록 성인이어도/성인이더라도/성인일지라도 담배는 피지 마라.
  Do not smoke even if you are an adult.
- ☐ 네가 미성년이 아니어도/아니더라도/아닐지라도 담배는 피지 마라.
  Do not smoke even though you are not a minor.
- ☐ 시간이 없어도/없더라도/없을지라도 서두르지 말자.
  Let's not hurry even if we don't have time.

5. Selection: ~거나, ~든, ~든지, ~든가

1. All connect clauses when selecting one clause from clauses which have different condition or situation.
2. All use "~았/었~" for 과거시제, but do not use "~겠~" for 미래시제.
3. 접속부사 of "또는" or "아니면" can be used together to emphasize the meaning of selection.
4. "~든" is 준말 of "~든지" and "~든가".

- ☐ 나는 방학 중에 바다에 가거나/가든지/가든가 (또는/아니면) 산에 간다.
  I go to sea or mountain during vacation.
- ☐ 밥을 먹든가 (또는/아니면) 빵을 먹든가 결정하자.
  Let's decide to eat rice or bread.
- ☐ 배구를 하거나 농구를 하거나 축구를 하거나 어느 것이 좋으냐?
  Which do you like to play volleyball, basketball or football?
- ☐ 집에 돌아가든가/돌아가든 말든가/말든 그것은 네 자유다.
  Whether you go home or not is up to you.
- ☐ 밥을 먹든지/먹든 빵을 먹든지/먹든 아무거나 먹어라.
  Eat anything, no matter rice or bread.
- ☐ 미국에 가든가/가든 일본에 가든가/가든 마음대로 해라.
  It is up to you to go to America or to Japan.
- ☐ 값이 비싸거나 싸거나 신경 안 쓴다.
  Expensive or inexpensive, I do not mind.
- ☐ 키가 크든/크든지/크든가 작든/작든지/작든가 상관없다.
  It doesn't matter, tall or small.

6. Method/Means: ~(아/어)서, ~고

1. Both connect the clauses when the preceding clause expresses method or means for the following clause.
2. Both do not use 선어말어미 for tense.
3. For both, 주어 of each clause should be same.
4. Both match with 동사 only.

- ▢ 우리는 배를 타고 제주도에 갔다.
  We went to Jeju Island by ship.
- ▢ 나는 물안경을 쓰고 수영을 했다.
  I swam with diver's glasses on.
- ▢ 비행기를 타고 제주도에 가자.
  Let's go to Jeju Island by airplane.
- ▢ 그는 열심히 일해서 부자가 되었다.
  He became rich through working hard.
- ▢ 어떻게 돼지고기를 요리해서 먹을까?
  How do we cook the pork to eat?
- ▢ 그들은 배를 타지 않고(←않다) 비행기를 타고 제주도에 갔다.
  They went to Jeju Island, not by ship but by airplane.

7. Background: ~ㄴ데/~는데/~은데, ~(으)니

1. Both connect the clauses when the preceding clause expresses the background in advance for explanation, question or suggestion in the following clause.

2 "~ㄴ데/~는데/~은데" uses "~았/었~" for 과거시제, but "~겠~" can not be used for 미래시제. When the person speaking expresses the situation at the moment, "~겠~" can be used.

- ☐ 어젯밤 배가 고파 죽겠는데(←죽다/die) 먹을 것이 없었다.
  I was unbearably hungry last night, but I had nothing to eat.
- ☐ 머리가 아파 미치겠는데(←미치다/become insane) 집에 두통약이 없다.
  My head hurts terribly, but there is no headache pill at home.

3 "~(으)니" uses "~았더니/었더니" for 과거시제 and doesn't use "~겠~" for 미래시제.

4 "~(으)니" does not match with 청유문, 명령문 at 부정문.

- ☐ 시장에 가는데 무엇을 살까?
  I am going to the market, so what shall I buy?
- ☐ 시간도 많은데/많으니 천천히 해라.
  You have a lot of time, so do it slowly.
- ☐ 그는 저의 친구인데 함께 일합니다.
  He is a friend of mine, who works with me, sir.
- ☐ 지난주에 친구 집을 방문했는데/방문했더니 집에 없었다.
  I visited a friend's house last week, but he was not.
- ☐ 현복이는 거기에 안 갔는데 너는 갔었느냐?
  Hyeonbok didn't go there, but did you go?
- ☐ 약을 먹었더니 감기가 치료되었다.
  Because I took the medicine, my cold was cured.
- ☐ 아침에 깨어났더니 이미 10시였다.
  Waking up in the morning, it was already 10 o'clock.
- ☐ 너는 올해 서른 살이니/살인데 결혼할 나이다.
  Since you are 30 years old this year, so it's the age to get married.

SECTION

23

유용한 표현들 I

Useful Expressions I

1. (용언)~ㄹ 수밖에 없다.: no other way but ~/can not help but ~/should ~

- ☐ 돈이 없어서 친구한테 빌릴 수밖에 없었다.
  Because of no money, there was no other way but to borrow from friend.
- ☐ 지금은 한여름이기 때문에 더울 수밖에 없다.
  Since it's midsummer now, it should be hot.
- ☐ 겨울에는 과일이 비쌀 수밖에 없다.
  During the winter, the fruits should be expensive.
- ☐ 나는 그렇게 할 수밖에 없었다.
  I had no other way but to do so.

2. (관형사/체언)~ 뿐만 아니라 (체언)~도 ~: not only ~ but also ~/~ as well as ~/neither ~ nor ~

- ☐ 그는 지혜로울 뿐만 아니라 겸손하기도 하다.
  He is not only wise but also humble.
- ☐ 영희는 예쁠 뿐만 아니라 똑똑하기도 하다.
  Yeonghi is not only beautiful but also clever.
- ☐ 나는 미국뿐만 아니라 영국도 자주 간다.
  I visit England often as well as America.
- ☐ 골프를 치려면 돈뿐만 아니라 시간도 많이 필요하다.
  Playing golf requires a lot of time as well as money.
- ☐ 그는 건강뿐만 아니라 재산도 없다.
  He has neither health nor wealth.

* When "뿐" is combined with 관형사, it is 의존명사. But when combined with 체언, it is 보조사 that should be written without space.

3. (용언/서술격조사)~아/어 봤자/보았자(←보다) ~: no use ~/even though ~

- ☐ 지금 역에 가 봤자/보았자 기차는 이미 떠났다.
  There is no use going to the station now, since the train has already left.
- ☐ 기차가 빨라 봤자 비행기보다 느리다.
  Even though the train is fast, but slower than airplane.
- ☐ 쏟아진 우유에 울어 보았자 소용없다.
  It is no use crying over spilt milk.
- ☐ 밤새워 기다려 봤자 네 친구는 안 온다.
  It is no use waiting for your friend whole night, since he will not come.
- ☐ 내가 회사 사장이어 봤자 직원은 겨우 두 명이다.
  Even though I'm a boss of a company, there are only two staffs.

* "봤자" is 준말 of "보았자".

4. (체언)~도 (체언)~도 아니다./없다.: neither ~ nor ~

- ☐ 그는 건강도 재산도 없다.
  He has neither health nor property.
- ☐ 나는 골프를 칠 시간도 돈도 없다.
  I have neither time nor money to play golf.
- ☐ 너도 나도 잘못이 없다.
  Neither you nor I am to blame.
- ☐ 그도 그녀도 아직 도착하지 않았다.
  Neither he nor she has arrived yet.
- ☐ 저 여자는 영희도 순희도 아니다.
  That woman is neither Yeonghi nor Sunhi.

5. (용언)~기보다(는) ~: better than/instead of/rather than ~

- [ ] 나는 공부하기보다(는) 운동하기를 더 좋아한다.
I like to exercise better than to study.

- [ ] 식당에서 먹기보다(는) 집에서 먹는 것이 더 좋다.
It's better to eat at home than to eat at a restaurant.

- [ ] 전화로 얘기하기보다(는) 직접 만나서 얘기하자.
Instead of talking on the phone, let's talk in person.

- [ ] 티브이 뉴스를 보기보다(는) 신문을 읽는 것이 더 좋다.
Reading newspaper is better than watching TV news.

- [ ] 철수는 영리하기보다(는) 열심히 공부하는 학생이다.
Cheolsu is a student who studies hard rather than smart.

- [ ] 나는 예쁘기보다(는) 현명한 여자가 좋다.
I like wise women rather than pretty woman.

* "~기보다는" implies the firmer intention of the person speaking than "~(기)보다".

6. (용언)~기만 하다.: continuous or persistent in a habit, a condition or a situation

- [ ] 아기가 계속해서 울기만 한다.
The baby just keeps crying only, Mr. ~.

- [ ] 어제는 피곤해서 하루 종일 자기만 했다.
Because tired yesterday, just only I slept all day long, Miss ~.

- [ ] 그 사람은 게으르기만 해서 싫다.
I don't like him because he's always lazy.

- [ ] 부지런하기만 하면 굶지는 않는다.
If only diligent, you don't starve.

- [ ] 저는 너무 배가 고파서 계속 먹기만 했습니다.
I kept eating only, because I was so hungry, madam.

7. (용언/서술격조사)~(이)거든(요).: because/since ~ (Mr. ~).

☐ A: 왜 늦었어?
Why are you late?

B: 비가 너무 많이 왔거든(←왔다←오다).
Because it rained so heavy.

☐ A: 왜 뚱뚱해졌어?
Why did you become fat?

B: 매일 맥주를 많이 마셨거든(←마셨다←마시다).
Because I drank much beer everyday.

☐ A: 테니스를 정말 잘 하시는군요!
You play tennis really well, Mrs. ~!

B: 학생이었을 때 테니스선수였(←이었)거든요.
Because I was a tennis player during school days, Mr. ~.

☐ A: 피곤해 보여요(←보이다←보다).
You look tired, Mr. ~.

B: 어젯밤 잠을 잘 못 잤거든(←잤다←자다).
Since I couldn't sleep well last night.

☐ A: 왜 이 식당에서 자주 식사하세요?
Why do you eat often in this restaurant, Mrs. ~?

B: 음식이 싸고 맛있거든(←맛있다).
Because the food is cheap and delicious.

8. (체언)~는/은 물론이고 (체언)~도/까지 ~: not only ~ but also ~/ as well as / neither ~ nor ~

☐ 식사는 물론이고 맥주도/맥주까지 내가 사겠다.
I'll buy not only food but also beer.

☐ 어제는 너무 바빠서 점심은 물론이고 저녁도/저녁까지 못 먹었다.
Yesterday I was so busy that I could eat neither lunch nor dinner.

☐ 우리 회사는 세 끼 식사는 물론이고 숙소도 제공한다.
Our company offers accommodation as well as three meals.

☐ 나는 너에게 음식은 물론이고 용돈까지 주겠다.
I will give you allowance as well as food.

9. (체안)~만 (용언)~(으)면 그만이다.: as long as ~, that's enough/ok.

☐ 부부 사이는 사랑하는 마음만 있으면 그만이다.
The relation of a couple is enough as long as they have a loving heart.

☐ 아이는 건강만 좋으면 그만이에요.
As long as the child's health is good, that's enough. Mr. ~.

☐ 학생은 공부만 잘 하면 그만이지/그만이야.
As long as the student is good at studying, that's enough.

* "그만이지." and "그만이야." express that the personal feeling of the person speaking is firmer than "그만이다."

☐ 인생은 마음만 편하면 그만입니다.
Only if the mind is peaceful in life, that's enough, sir.

☐ 우리 회사는 영어만 잘 하면 그만이지요./그만이죠.
In our company as long as English-speaking is good, that's enough, Miss ~.

* "그만이지요." is the colloquial 존댓말 of "그만이지." Instead of "~이지요.", "~이죠." is also used often as 준말.

10. (용언/서술격조사)~잖아(요).: As you know ~/Because ~, (Mrs. ~)

- [ ] A: 어디 가세요?
  Where are you going, Mr. ~?

  B: 산책하러 가요. 날씨가 좋잖아요.
  I'm going for a walk. Because the weather is nice, Mrs. ~.

- [ ] 맥주 한 잔 하자. 여름에는 시원한 맥주가 최고잖아.
  Let's have a glass of beer. Because the cold beer is the best in summer.

- [ ] 왜 늦었어? 한 시부터 회의가 시작하잖아.
  Why are you late? As you know, the meeting starts at one o'clock.

- [ ] 너무 야단치지 마세요. 영수는 아직 초등학생이잖아요.
  Don't berate too much, Mr. ~. As you know, Yeongsu is still in elementary school.

11. (용언/서술격조사]~ㄹ(을) 텐데 ~: I guess ~, (so) ~/I think ~, (so) ~

- [ ] 배가 고플 텐데 우선 식사부터 하세요.
  I think, you are hungry, (so) eat first, Mr. ~.

- [ ] 내일은 더울 텐데 바다에 수영하러 가자.
  I guess, it will be hot tomorrow, (so) let's go swimming in the sea.

- [ ] 영호는 어제 서울에 갔을 텐데 전화해 보자.
  I think, Yeongho went to Seoul yesterday, (so) let's call him.

- [ ] 아직 학생일 텐데 공부 열심히 해라.
  I guess, you are still a student, (so) study hard.

12. (용언/서술격조사) ~기는(요)!: Nope!/Not so ~! ~ (Mr. ~).

☐ A: 정말 부지런하구나!
How industrious you are!

B: 부지런하기는! 오늘 아침은 9시에 일어났어.
Nope! I woke up at nine in the morning today.

☐ A: 요리를 참 잘 하는구나!
You really cook well!

B: 잘 하기는! 그냥 요리책을 따라하고 있어.
Nope! I am just following the cookbook.

* "아드님" is 높임표현 of "아들/son".
* 높임표현 of "딸/daughter" is "따님".

☐ A: 아드님이 참 잘 생겼습니다.
How handsome your son is, sir!

B: 잘 생기기는요! 잘 봐 주셔서 감사합니다.
Not so handsome! Thank you for your kind compliment, sir.

☐ A: 부자여(←부자이어)서 좋겠군요.
It's good because you're rich. Mr. ~..

B: 부자(이)기는요. 집 한 채밖에 없어요.
Not that rich, huh! Just a house to me, Mrs. ~.

13. (용언)~아야지(요)./~어야지(요).: should/need ~, (Mr. ~).

☐ A: 늦어서 미안해.
Sorry to be late.

B: 늦지 않으려면 더 일찍 출발했어야지.
In order not to be late, you should have depart earlier.

☐ A: 담배를 정말 많이 피우는군요!
You smoke really a lot, Mr. ~!

B: 담배 피워서 미안해요. 줄여야지요./줄여야죠.(←줄이다)
Sorry to smoke. I should reduce, Mrs. ~.

- [ ] A: 엄마, 커피를 마셔서 잠이 안 와요.
  Because I drank coffee, I can not get to sleep, mom.

  B: 그러면 자기 전에 커피를 마시지 말았어야지.
  If so, you shouldn't drink coffee before going to bed.

- [ ] A: 요즈음 몸이 약해진 것 같애(←같다).
  I feel my body is weaker these days.

  B: 건강해지려면 매일 운동을 해야지.
  You need to exercise everyday to be healthy.

14. (동사)~곤 하다: once in a while/occasionally

- [ ] 저는 기분이 우울하면 이 공원에서 산책하곤 합니다.
  I take a walk in this park once in a while when I'm depressed, sir.
- [ ] 이 식당에서 가족과 함께 식사를 하곤 한다.
  Occasionally I eat with family at this restaurant.
- [ ] 독일에서 살 때, 라인강을 따라 자전거를 타곤 했다.
  Occasionally I cycled along the Rhine, while living in Germany.
- [ ] 나는 퇴근할 때, 이 가게에서 과일을 사곤 했다.
  Once in a while I bought fruits at this store when I went home from work.

15. (동사)~(을)ㄹ 걸 그랬다.: should have done ~/ It's regrettable not to have done ~

- 이 집은 너무 작아요. 더 큰 집을 살 걸 그랬어요.
  This house is too small. I should have bought a bigger house, Mr ~.
- 버스는 너무 느립니다. 지하철을 탈 걸 그랬습니다.
  The bus is too slow. It's regrettable not to have ridden the subway, sir.
- 아이고! 버스는 벌써 떠났구나. 더 빨리 올 걸 그랬다./그랬어.
  Oh my! The bus has already left. We should have come earlier.
- 불고기보다 생선회를 먹을 걸 그랬다./그랬어.
  We should have eaten raw fish rather than bulgogi.

16. (용언/서술격조사)~(을)ㄹ 테니까: because ~/so ~

- 지금 갈 테니까, 기다리세요.
  Because I go now, please wait.
- 오후에 비가 올 테니까, 우산을 가지고 가거라.
  It's going to rain in the afternoon, so take an umbrella with you.
- 어제 일 하느라고 힘들었을 테니까, 오늘은 쉬어라.
  Take a rest today since you woked hard time yesterday.
- 그때는 아이였을 테니까, 너는 정치에 대해서 몰랐겠지.
  I guess, you didn't know about politics since you were a kid at that time.
- 과일을 보낼 테니까, 맛있게 드세요.
  I will send you fruit, so enjoy it, Mr. ~.

17. (용언/서술격조사)~지만/~기는 하지만: although / agree ~, but ~

- [ ] 한국산 제품이 다소 비싸지만/비싸기는 하지만 품질이 매우 좋다.
I agree that Korean products are relatively expensive but the quality is very good.

- [ ] 이 신발은 비싸지만/비싸기는 하지만 쉽게 떨어진다.
These shoes are expensive, but wear out easily.

- [ ] 방이 컸지만/크기는 했지만 깨끗하지 않아서 싫었다.
Although the room was spacious, I didn't like it because not clean.

- [ ] 맥주를 마시지만/마시기는 하지만 좋아하지 않는다.
Although I drink beer, I don't like it.

- [ ] 저는 한국인이지만/한국인이기는 하지만 매운 음식을 잘 못 먹어요.
I'm Korean, but can't eat spicy food well, Mr. ~.

SECTION

24

유용한 표현들 II

Useful Expressions II

1.

(동사)~(을)ㄹ 만하다.: be worth/deserve

☐ 한국음식은 맵지만 먹을 만하다.
Korean food is spicy but worth eating.

☐ 그의 행위는 칭찬받을 만합니다.
His act deserves praise, sir.

☐ 그는 믿을 만한 사람이다.
He is a trustworthy man.

☐ 제주도는 경치가 아름다워서 여행할 만하다.
Jeju Island has beautiful scenery, so it is worth traveling.

☐ 이 책은 읽을 만하다.
This book is worth reading.

* "만" of "만하다" is 의존명사.

2.

(용언)~(을)ㄹ 정도~: so ~ to ~/so ~ that ~

☐ 나는 영희와 어깨가 닿을 정도로 가깝게 걸었다.
I walked with Yeonghi so close that my shoulder touches her shoulder.

☐ 나는 때려(→ 때리다/hit, slap, beat) 주고 싶을 정도로 승기가 밉다.
Seunggi is so hateful that I feel like beating him.

☐ 나는 아이스크림을 매우 좋아해서 매일 먹을 정도이다.
I like ice cream so much that I eat it every day.

☐ 우리 가족은 노래하기를 좋아해서 집에 노래방 기계가 있을 정도이다.
My family loves to sing so much to have a karaoke machine at home.

3. (~면) (용언/서술격조사) ~ㄹ(을/일)수록 더 ~: the more ~, the more ~

- ☐ 벼는 (익으면) 익을수록 고개를 더 숙인다.
  The more the rice ripens, the more it bows.
- ☐ 사람은 (배우면) 배울수록 더 겸손하다.
  The more learned a person is, the humbler he is.
- ☐ 김치는 (익으면) 익을수록 더 맛있다.
  The more fermented Kimchi is, the more delicious it is.
- ☐ 너를 (보면) 볼수록 더 보고 싶다.
  The more I see you, the more I want to see you.
- ☐ (부자이면/부자면) 부자일수록 더 절약한다.
  The richer, the more thrifty.

4. (동사)~았다/었다 하면 항상 ~: Once/if ~, always/usually ~

- ☐ BTS가 공연을 했다 하면 공연장은 항상 만원이다.
  Once BTS gives a performance, the venue is always full.
- ☐ 저는 무엇이든지 시작했다 하면 항상 끝을 냅니다.
  Once I start anything, I finish it always, sir.
- ☐ 나는 필리핀에 갔다 하면 항상 반년씩 머무른다.
  Once I went to the Philippines, I stay usually for a half year.
- ☐ 정수는 친구와 통화를 했다 하면 항상 한 시간이다.
  Once Jeongsu calls a friend, he usually talks for an hour.

5. (동사)~(으)려던 참에 ~: at the moment of(to) ~ /When(As) ~ be about to ~

☐ (막) 떠나려던 참에 소나기가 왔다.
It showered when I was (just) at the moment of leaving.

☐ 여행을 가려던 참에 할아버지가 돌아가셔서 여행을 취소했다.
My grandfather passed away at the momemt to start a trip, so I canceled it.

☐ 시장에 (막) 가려던 참에 친구가 와서 함께 가는 중이다.
I'm on the way to the market with a friend because he visited me (just) at the moment of going to the market.

☐ 밥을 막 먹으려던 참에 전화가 왔다.
As I was just about to eat, I got a phone call.

* "막" is 부사 which emphasizes the moment. → Section 18

6. (동사)~다가는 ~: if continue ~

☐ 그렇게 게으르게 공부하다가는 시험에 떨어지겠다.
If you continue to study so sluggish, maybe you will fail in the exam.

☐ 그렇게 담배를 많이 피우다가는 폐암에 걸린다.
If you continue to smoke so much, you will suffer from lung cancer.

☐ 우산 없이 비를 맞다가는 감기에 걸린다.
If you continue to be exposed to rain without umbrella, you will catch a cold.

☐ 매일 그렇게 많이 먹다가는 뚱보가 된다.
If you to continue to eat so much every day, you will become fat.

☐ 이렇게 혼자 살다가는 우울증에 걸릴 것 같다.
If I continue to live alone like this, I might suffer from mental depression.

7. (용언/서술격조사)~(을)ㄹ지도 모른다.: maybe ~/not sure ~

- [ ] 공부를 열심히 안 해서 시험에 떨어질지도 몰라요./모르죠.
  Maybe I fail in the test, because I didn't study hard, Mr. ~.
- [ ] 나는 내일 학교에 못 갈지도 몰라./모르지
  I'm not sure that I can not go to school tomorrow.
- [ ] 이 아이는 대통령이 될지도 모른다.
  We are not sure that this kid become the President.
- [ ] 그 남자는 아직 총각일지도 모른다.
  Maybe that man is still a bachelor.
- [ ] 지하철이 택시보다 느릴지도 몰라요.
  Maybe the subway is slower than taxi, Mr. ~.

8. (용언/서술격조사)~ㄴ/~ㄹ 것/거 같다: look like ~/I guess ~/be likely ~/seem ~/maybe ~

* Expression for assumption or uncertain conclusion
* "것/거" means "thing, fact, phenomenon, event, etc. as 의존명사. "거" is colloquial and "것" is literary.

- [ ] 내일 비가 올 것/거 같습니다.
  It looks like it will rain tomorrow, sir.
- [ ] 어젯밤에 비가 온 것/거 같다.
  It seems that it rained last night.
- [ ] 그는 지금 공원에서 산책을 하고 있는 것/거 같다.
  He seems to have a walk in the park now.
- [ ] 지하철을 탔으면 더 빨리 도착했을 거 같다.
  If I had taken the subway, maybe I would have arrived earlier.

☐ 영희는 자라면 예쁠 것 같다.
I guess that Yeonghi will be pretty when she grows up.

☐ 엄마, 저 사람은 한국 사람인 거 같아요.(→ 사람 같아요.)
It seems to me that he is a Korean, mom.

☐ 그 사람은 간첩인 것 같아서(→ 간첩 같아서) 경찰에 신고했어요.
Because the man looked like a spy, I reported him to the police, Mr. ~.

* In case for 체언, "같다" is used as predicative adjective and as 형용사적 관형사.
- 그는 간첩 같다.: He looks like a spy.
  간첩 같은 사람: a man like a spy
- 그 이야기는 거짓말 같다.: The story is like a lie
  거짓말 같은 이야기: a story like a lie
- 그는 실업자 같았다.: He looked like an unemployed.
  실업자 같았던 사람: a person who looked like an unemployed

9. (용언/서술격조사)~면서(요)?: I heard/know ~, right/is it true, (Mr. ~)?

☐ 어제 영국에서 돌아왔다면서요?
I heard that you came back from England yesterday, is it true, Mr. ~?

☐ 너는 어제 영희랑 영화 봤다면서?
I heard you watched a movie with Yeonghi yesterday, right?

☐ 일본으로 여행할거라면서요?
I heard you're going to travel to Japan, right, uncle?

☐ 영희는 아주 착하다면서요?
I know Yeonghi is very kind, right, Mrs. ~?

☐ 영희는 아직 학생이라면서?
I know that Yeonghi is still a student, is it true?

10. (용언/서술격조사)~더라(~더라고요).: I noticed/realized/found ~, (Mr. ~).

- [ ] 영희는 집에서 공부를 하고 있더라고요.
  I found that Yeonghi was studying at home, Mr. ~.
- [ ] 공원에 사람들이 많더라.
  I found that there were a lot of people in the park.
- [ ] 집에 아무도 없더라고요.
  I noticed that nobody was at home, Mrs. ~.
- [ ] 아기가 초콜릿을 맛있게 먹더라.
  I noticed that the baby was eating chocolate deliciously.
- [ ] 순희는 아직 초등학생이더라.
  I noticed that Sunhi was still in elementary school.
- [ ] 시험이 매우 어렵더라.
  I realized that the examination was very difficult.

11. (용언)~ㄴ(은) 대신 ~/(체언) 대신 ~: instead ~

- [ ] 밥을 먹는 대신 빵을 먹겠다.
  I will eat bread instead of rice.
- [ ] 품질이 좋은 대신 가격이 비싸다.
  The price is high instead the quality is good.
- [ ] 오늘은 동생 대신 내가 방을 청소한다.
  Today I clean the room instead of my brother.
- [ ] 내일은 내 대신 동생이 방을 청소할 것이다.
  Tomorrow my brother will clean the room instead of me.

12. (체언)~은/는 고사하고/~은커녕/는커녕 (체언)~도/~조차 없다./아니다.
: far from ~, not even ~/neither ~ nor ~

- [ ] 저축은커녕/저축은 고사하고 쌀 살 돈도/돈조차 없다.
Far from saving money, I don't money even to buy rice.

- [ ] 예쁘기는 고사하고/예쁘기는커녕 성격조차/성격도 나쁘다.
Far from being pretty, even the character is bad.

- [ ] 해외여행은 고사하고/해외여행은커녕 제주도조차/제주도도 가지 못한다.
Far from traveling abroad, I can not go even to Jejudo.

- [ ] 아파트는 고사하고/아파트는커녕 허름한 집조차/집도 없다.
Far from an apartment, I do not have even a shedlike cottage.

- [ ] 오토바이는 고사하고/오토바이는커녕 자전거조차/자전거도 없다.
I have neither a motorcycle, nor even a bike.

13. (동명사)~기 십상이다.:
be prone/easy/liable to ~

- [ ] 밤늦게 식사를 하면 살이 찌기 십상이다./십상이지.
Eating late at night is prone to gain the weight.

- [ ] 말을 안 하면 오해받기 십상입니다.
If you do not speak, you are liable to be misunderstood, sir.

- [ ] 일하다가 졸면 다치기 십상이지요./십상이죠.
It's liable to get injured if you doze off over work, Mr. ~.

- [ ] 교통신호를 안 지키면 사고를 내기 십상이다./십상이지.
If you don't obey the traffic signals, it's easy to cause an accident.

- [ ] 혼자 멋대로 하면 문제가 발생하기 십상이지요./십상이죠.
If man does alone as he likes, it's liable to cause problems, Mrs. ~.

14. (용언/서술격조사)~ㄴ데도 불구하고/(체언)~에도 불구하고: despite/although~

- ☐ 영희는 예쁜데도 불구하고 남자친구가 없다.
  Although Yeonghi is pretty, she does not have a boyfriend,
- ☐ 선생님, 저는 열심히 공부하는데도 불구하고 시험성적이 나빠요.
  I have a bad test score despite studying hard, ma'am.
- ☐ 부모님의 강한 반대에도 불구하고 영희와 결혼했다.
  Despite the parents' strong objections, I married Yeonghi.
- ☐ 오랜 다이어트에도 불구하고 살이 빠지지 않는다.
  In spite of a long diet I do not lose weight.
- ☐ 영수는 게으른데도 불구하고 시험결과가 좋다.
  Although Yeongsu is lazy, the test scores are good.

15. (체언)~을 막론하고: regardless of ~/for whatever ~

- ☐ 제주도는 남녀노소를 막론하고 여행하기 좋은 곳이다.
  Jejudo is a good place to travel regardless of age or gender.
- ☐ 이번 사고는 이유를 막론하고 자세히 조사해야 한다.
  This incident should be investigated in detail for whatever reason.
- ☐ 그 영화배우는 나이를 막론하고 모든 사람이 좋아한다.
  The movie star is loved by all people regardless of age.

16.

(체언)~을/를 무릅쓰고: despite ~/in defiance of ~

- [ ] 소방관들은 위험을 무릅쓰고 불을 끈다.
  Firefighters put out the fire despite the danger.
- [ ] 군인은 죽음의 위험을 무릅쓰고 적과 싸운다.
  The soldiers fight the enemy despite the danger of death.
- [ ] 나는 추위를 무릅쓰고 한라산에 올라갔다.
  I climbed Mount Halla despite the cold.

17.

(동사)~ㄹ 여지가 있다.(없다.): There is (no) room for ~

- [ ] 우리 회사는 아직 개선할 여지가 있다.
  There is still room for improvement in our company.
- [ ] 이 사건에 대해서는 의심할 여지가 있다.
  There is room for doubt about this affair.
- [ ] 이 문제에 대해서 더 이상 논쟁할 여지가 없다.
  There is no more room to argue further about this problem.
- [ ] 제 실수이기 때문에 변명할 여지가 없습니다.
  There is no room to excuse for me because it is my mistake, sir.
- [ ] 나는 그들의 토론에 참가할 여지가 없었다.
  There was no room for me to participate in their discussion.

18. (용언) ~도록 (동사)~하다

1 to the time when ~, till ~, until ~

☐ 그는 항상 밤 늦도록(←늦다) 공부한다.
He studies always till late at night.

☐ 나는 그녀를 죽도록(←죽다) 사랑했다.
I loved her to death.

☐ 나의 할아버지는 백 살이 되도록(←되다) 사셨다(←사시다←살다).
My grandfather lived to be a hundred.

☐ 너무 재미있어서 눈물이 나도록(←나다) 웃었다,
Because so funny, I laughed untill the tears ran down my face.

2 in order to/so that ~

☐ 그런 일이 없도록(←없다) 조심해라.
Be careful so that such a thing will not happen.

☐ 부모는 아이들이 건강하게 자라도록(←자라다) 보살핀다.
Parents take care of their children so that they grow up healthy.

☐ 기차 시간에 늦지 않도록(←않다) 일찍 일어났다.
I got up early in order not to be late for the train.

* "~도록 하다" can be used in stead of 보조동사(~게 하다) in 사동문.

나는 아이들을 정원에서 놀게 했다./놀도록 했다.
I let my children play in the garden.

나는 아들을 일찍 학교에 가게 했다./가도록 했다.
I have my son go to school early.

Appendix

문법 용어

Terms for Grammar

1. 알파벳, 자모: Alphabet

- 발음: Pronunciation
- 읽기: Reading
- 자음: Consonant
  - 단자음: Single consonant
  - 쌍자음: Twin consonant
  - 받침자음: Final consonant
  - 겹받침: Final double consonant
  - 평음: Plain sound
  - 경음: Strong sound
  - 격음: Aspirate sound
- 모음: Vowel
  - 단모음: Single vowel
  - 이중모음: Double vowel
  - 중간모음: Medial vowel
- Sounds from each part of mouth
  - 아음: Sound from molar teeth
  - 설음: Sound from tongue
  - 순음: Sound from lips
  - 치음: Sound from front teeth
  - 후음: Sound from throat
- Phonemic element of 음절
  - 초성: Initial sound
  - 중성: Medial sound
  - 종성: Final sound
- Voiced and voiceless sound
  - 유성음: voiced sound
  - 유성자음: voiced consonant
  - 무성음: voiceless sound
  - 무성자음: voiceless consonant

- 글자, 문자: letter, character

2. Word as an element for structure of sentence

- 단어, 낱말: Word
  - 음절: Syllable
  - 어간: Word-stem
  - 어미: Word-ending
    - 연결어미: Connective word-ending
    - 종결어미: Terminative word-ending
    - 선어말어미: Preceding word-ending
    - 어말어미: Final word-ending
  - 어근: Word-root
  - 접사: Affix
    - 접두사: Prefix
    - 접미사: Suffix
    - 삽입사: Infix
- 주어: Subject(S)
- 서술어: Predicate(P)
- 보어: Complement(C)
- 목적어: Object(O)
- 부사어: Adverbial word(AW)
- 준말: Abbreviated word
- 본딧말: Original word

3. 품사: Part of speech

- 명사: Noun
  - 자립명사: Independent noun
  - 의존명사: Incomplete noun
  - 고유명사: Proper noun
  - 보통명사: Common noun
  - 추상명사: Abstract noun
  - 물질명사: Material noun
  - 파생명사: Derivative noun
  - 복합명사: Compound noun
  - 동명사: Gerund
  - 형용명사: Adjectival noun
  - 단음절명사: Monosyllabic noun
- 대명사: Pronoun
  - 인칭대명사: Personal pronoun
  - 지시대명사: Demonstrative pronoun
  - 의문대명사: Interrogative pronoun
- 수사: Numeral
  - 기수: Cardinal number
  - 서수: Ordinal number
- 조사: Postposition(PP)
  - 격조사: PP for case
    - 주격조사: Subjective PP
    - 목적격조사: Objective PP
    - 보격조사: Complementary PP
    - 관형격조사: Pre-nominal PP
    - 부사격조사: Adverbial PP
    - 서술격조사: Predicative PP
    - 호격조사: Vocative PP
  - 보조사: Auxiliary PP
- 동사: Verb
  - 자동사: Intransitive verb
    - 완전자동사: Complete intransitive verb
    - 불완전자동사: Incomplete intransitive verb
  - 타동사: Transitive verb
    - 완전타동사: Complete transitive verb
    - 불완전타동사: Incomplete transitive verb
    - 수여동사: Dative verb
    - 사역동사: Causative verb
  - 보조동사: Auxiliary verb
  - 능동사: Active verb
  - 피동사: Passive verb
  - 규칙동사: Regular verb
  - 불규칙동사: Irregular verb
  - 파생동사: Derived verb
- 형용사: Adjective
  - 규칙형용사: Regular adjective
  - 불규칙형용사: Irregular adjective
  - 보조형용사: Auxiliary adjective
  - 쌍음절형용사: Twinsyllabic adjective
  - 파생형용사: Derived adjective
- 관형사: Pre-noun
  - 수관형사: Numeral pre-noun
  - 지시관형사: Demonstrative pre-noun
  - 소유격관형사: Genitive(Possessive) pre-noun
  - 성상관형사: Specifying pre-noun
    - 순수관형사: Pure pre-noun
    - 동사적 관형사: Verbal pre-noun
    - 형용사적 관형사: Adjectival pre-noun
- 부사: Adverb
  - 성분부사: Adverb as element of sentence
  - 문장부사: Adverb for whole sentence
  - 파생부사: Derived adverb
  - 접속부사: Conjunctive adverb
  - 의문부사: Interrogative adverb
- 감탄사: Exclamation

4. Classification of 품사 according to the function in sentence

- 체언(명사, 대명사, 수사): Indeclinable word(noun, pronoun, numeral)
- 관계언(조사): Connective word(postposition)
- 용언(동사, 형용사): Declinable word(verb, adjective)
- 수식언(관형사, 부사): Modifying word(pre-noun, adverb)
- 독립언(감탄사): Independent word(exclamation)

5. 시제: Tense

- 현재시제: Present tense
- 과거시제: Past tense
- 대과거시제: Past perfect tense
- 미래시제: Future tense
  - 단순미래: Simple future
  - 의지미래: Volitional future

6. 문장: Sentence

- Classification of sentences
  - 평서문: Declarative sentence
  - 의문문: Interrogative sentence
  - 명령문: Imperative sentence
  - 청유문: Let's-sentence
  - 감탄문: Exclamatory sentence
- 서법: Mood
  - 직설법: Indicative mood
  - 가정법: Subjunctive mood
  - 명령법: Imperative mood
- 태: Voice
  - 능동태: Active voice
  - 수동태: Passive voice
- 화법: Speech/Narration
  - 직접화법: Direct speech
  - 간접화법: Indirect speech
- Style of speech
  - 구어체: Colloquial style
  - 문어체: Literary style
- Form of sentence
  - 단문: Simple sentence
  - 중문: Compound sentence
  - 복문: Complex sentence
    - 주절: Main clause
    - 종속절: Subordinate clause
- Five formulas of sentence structure
  - Formula 1(1 형식): S(주어) + P(서술어)
  - Formula 2(2 형식): S(주어) + C(보어) +P(서술어)
  - Formula 3(3 형식): S(주어) + AW(부사어) + P(서술어)
  - Formula 4(4 형식): S(주어) + O(목적어) + P(서술어)
  - Formula 5(5 형식): S(주어) + AW(부사어) + O(목적어) + P(서술어)

7. Grammatical signs

- 마침표/점: .(period)
- 쉼표/콤마: ,(comma)
- 따옴표/인용부호(quotation marks)
  - 큰 따옴표: " "(double quotation marks)
  - 작은 따옴표: ' '(single quotation marks)
- 느낌표: !(exclamation mark)
- 물음표: ?(question mark)
- 괄호: ( )(parentheses)
- 중괄호: [ ](braces)
- 연자부호: -(hyphen)
- 콜론: :(colon)
- 세미콜론: ;(semi-colon)
- 사선: /(slash)

출판사, 저자, 강사, 독자가 공존하기 위한 문예림 정책

평등한 기회와 공정한 정책으로

올바른 출판문화를 이끌도록 하겠습니다.

저 자

1 도서의 판매부수에 따라 인세를 정산하지 않습니다.

우리는 도서 판매여부와 관계없이 초판, 증쇄 발행 후 30일 이내 일괄 지급합니다. 보다 좋은 콘텐츠 연구에 집중해주십시오. 판매보고는 반기별로, 증쇄 계획은 인쇄 60일 전 안내합니다.

2 도서 계약은 매절로 진행하지 않습니다.

매절계약은 불합리한 계약방식입니다. 이러한 방식은 저자들의 집필 의욕을 저해시키며, 결국에는 생존력 짧은 도서로 전락하고 맙니다.

3 판매량을 기준으로 절판하지 않습니다.

판매량에 따라 지속 판매 여부를 결정하지 않으며 전문성, 영속성, 희소성을 기준으로 합니다.

강 사

1 동영상강의 콘텐츠 계약은 매절로 진행하지 않습니다.

우리는 강사님의 소중한 강의를 일괄 취득하는 행위는 하지 않으며, 반기별 판매보고 후 정산합니다.

2 유료 동영상강의 인세는 콘텐츠 순 매출액의 20%를 지급합니다.(자사 사이트 기준)

우리는 가르침의 의미를 소중히 알며, 강사와 공존을 위하여 업계 최고 조건으로 진행합니다.

3 판매량에 따라 동영상강의 서비스를 중단하지 않습니다.

판매량에 따라 서비스 제공 여부를 결정하지 않으며 지속가능한 의미가 있다면 유지합니다. 전문성, 영속성, 희소성을 기준으로 합니다.

독자 및 학습자

1 도서는 제작부수에 따라 정가를 정합니다.

적절한 정가는 저자가 지속적인 연구할 수 있는 기반이 되며, 이를 통해 독자와 학습자에게 전문성 있는 다양한 콘텐츠로 보답할 것입니다.

2 도서 관련 음원(MP3)은 회원가입 없이 무료제공됩니다.

원어민 음원은 어학학습에 반드시 필요한 부분으로 아무런 제약 없이 자유롭게 제공합니다. 회원가입을 하시면 보다 많은 서비스와 정보를 얻으실 수 있습니다.

3 모든 콘텐츠는 책을 기반으로 합니다.

우리의 모든 콘텐츠는 책에서부터 시작합니다. 필요한 언어를 보다 다양한 콘텐츠로 제공하도록 하겠습니다.